I0149874

Getting Rich in Dubai Is Easy

Salem Al-Falasi

Copyright © 2016 by Salem Al-Falasi, DBA

All rights reserved. This book or any portion thereof may not be reproduced or used in any manner whatsoever without the express written permission of the publisher except for the use of brief quotations in a book review.

ISBN: 9948025423

ISBN: 978-9948-02-542-9

salemalfalasi.com

Although the author and publisher have made every effort to ensure that the information in this book was correct at press time, the author and publisher do not assume and hereby disclaim any liability to any party for any loss, damage, or disruption caused by errors or omissions, whether such errors or omissions result from negligence, accident, or any other cause.

Author photograph by Hamda Alfalasi

Contents

Introduction

There is a gigantic difference between earning a great deal of money and being rich.

—Marlene Dietrich

What does it mean to be "rich"? For some, it means having a great deal of money. For others, it means having an abundance of other things. Being rich might mean having an abundance of love and good people in your life. Perhaps it is having the freedom to travel or being in good health. Or maybe it means living the quiet life you've always wanted, free from the hustle and bustle of the busy world.

Being rich is really all about perspective. We all want different things, so it is safe to say that the cure-all to ensure a rich life is nonexistent. However, regardless of your personal wealth ideal, we can concur that financial freedom is important to everyone.

Yes, financial freedom. That's what this book is about. It's about the real reason many people never achieve financial freedom in their lifetimes. It's about changing your life philosophy. It's about discovering the true path to financial success and following this path to a rich, abundant life.

When you change your philosophy, everything changes. The book that you hold in your hands does not contain a list of steps or guidelines to getting rich; I give you something more valuable than that. I present to you the keys to changing your philosophy of life, which will inevitably change your financial well-being. When your philosophy changes, your standards change. Average will no longer be good enough for you. OK is not going to be acceptable. No, not for you.

People often speak of Dubai as the land where you can turn your financial dreams into reality. Why? They say that in Dubai, everything you need to achieve financial success is already in place: ample infrastructure, security, capital, and an open market. It is easy to become rich in Dubai. All you have to do is take action, snap up those opportunities, be the early bird, and get that juicy worm. Right?

You read, "It is easy to become rich in Dubai." But what do we mean by "easy"? Something easy is something that can be done without difficulty because it is simple or perhaps because someone else has already laid the groundwork. *OK*, you wonder, *if it's so easy to be rich in Dubai, then why are there so many without financial freedom?*

There is a good reason for this: These people aren't doing the right things. They are going through life with the wrong philosophy, or they have the correct philosophy yet neglect to apply it to their own lives (which I find distressing).

This book describes, in detail, the life-changing philosophy that will change your financial status. We'll explore this philosophy in great detail, and you will come to understand the various facets of a renewed way of thinking.

But before we delve in, let me introduce myself. My name is Salem Al-Falasi.

My life started out rather unremarkably. Like many of my peers, I studied business in school. As a 2008 graduate of the University of Dubai, I thought that my bachelor's degree in business administration was enough. By enough, I mean enough of a credential to graduate from my job as a police officer for Dubai Immigration and move on to something that would enrich my life and give me more financial freedom. You see, as a police officer working in the Dubai airport, I regularly observed individuals of varying degrees of wealth coming in and out of the United Arab Emirates. Taking a cue from these affluent people, I flew to the United States to study finance. After obtaining my master's degree from Webster University, I returned home to work for Du Telecommunications Company. It was a run-of-the-mill auditing job, to be honest. My desk was on the fortieth floor of Al Salam Tower in Dubai Internet City. "Al Salam" means "the peace." So I worked in Peace Tower. From the fortieth-floor window, it was peaceful, in a sense—peaceful because I could look out and see yachts dotting the sea, slowly moving along as the hours passed. But it was also disturbing and agitating to look back at my office and wonder, *Why am I not out there living the life I want? Why am I working from nine to six, five days a week, in a position that doesn't fulfill me?* These questions kept bugging me—until I finally left Peace Tower in 2014.

My life has changed quite drastically since then. After earning a PhD from the University of Liverpool, I now manage my own portfolio of companies in Dubai. I am financially free. But my financial freedom was not won with degrees, luck, or random good ideas and hard work. My financial freedom arose from a shift in my mind-set. I stopped lying to myself. I found and eliminated the negative mental blocks to my progress. I committed to becoming a better person every single day. That has made all the difference for me, and it will for you too.

Currently, I am fortunate to be a guest lecturer at various universities around the United Arab Emirates. My experience as a teacher and mentor has influenced me to write this book in the hopes that you, too, may find financial freedom and enjoy a "rich" life.

General Outline and Summary

In the first chapter, we will dispel the myths that all of Dubai's wealth comes from oil and examine the real sources of affluence in the emirate.

The second chapter explores the reasons why people do not become rich. We take an in-depth look at how their own philosophies hold them back. This includes the following:

- Complaining and blaming: It's easy to complain or blame others for why something isn't the way we want it. Complaining and blaming get us nowhere, but many people get stuck in one of these traps.
- Opportunity: Many fail to seize opportunities. There are many reasons for this, but the biggest one we will discuss (and the one that many excuses boil down to) is fear.
- Procrastination: Why do so many put off to tomorrow what can be done today? Many people do not take their pursuit of financial freedom seriously. They mistakenly think, *I'll do it tomorrow. It doesn't matter. It's really a small thing. It will not affect anything if I wait and open my dream business next year.*

The remaining chapters of this book will take you through each aspect of my philosophy, starting with a general introduction in chapter 3. This must-have philosophy will bring you financial success. What does the philosophy entail? We will discuss

- how to use your imagination and vision to create your reality;
- how to use motivation to get moving;
- how to change your thinking;
- how to use your negative emotions to push you forward;
- how to take action; and
- how to check in and assess your success along the way.

Now, some of you may be wondering, *Dubai? I don't live in Dubai. What does this have to do with me?* It's true that this is a book about getting rich in Dubai. However, the topics I discuss in the following pages are applicable to any situation, no matter where you live. How does that sound?

Ready for a massive change?

Good. Now pour yourself a nice cup of tea or coffee, and enjoy this book. I look forward to taking you on this journey.

Chapter 1: About Dubai

I want Dubai to be a place where everybody from all over the world meets one another, don't think of fighting or hate, just love it, enjoy their sport, and that's it.

—Mohammed bin Rashid Al Maktoum

Dubai. It is a land of opportunity for so many people. Long known to have achieved its wealthy image from its natural resources, particularly oil, Dubai has a different side to its wealth that few might be aware of. The state realized three decades ago that oil was not going to be enough to sustain the wealth of the city far into the future, so they set out to invest in other industries. The result was booming real-estate, finance, and tourist industries.

In this chapter, we will take a look at what makes Dubai tick and a few of the reasons why people have the opportunity to become wealthy there. We will also take a look at what can negatively affect a person's lifestyle when living in Dubai and what you need to plan for. This is not the primary focus of this book, but it gives you an idea of the setting in which you can apply the principles provided herein so you can get ahead of the game.

Dubai's History

The fact is that Dubai never really had a lot of riches from the oil industry. That privilege was primarily for Abu Dhabi. Dubai was a fairly autonomous member of the United Arab Emirates prior to 1996, when it integrated more fully into the United Arab Emirates, and it relied on its position as a port city for much of the wealth it did have. Traditionally, Dubai's economy was focused on fishing and trade with Persian Gulf partners, particularly with India. In fact, the trade and economic ties between Dubai and India go back as far as 3000 BC. The primary commodities traded from India to Dubai have been gemstones and precious metals, followed by oil. The primary commodities traded from Dubai to India are oil, followed by gemstones and precious metals. Today, India is still a top trading partner with Dubai.

But Dubai has a history of not conforming to the norm set by the other monarchies that form the United Arab Emirates. As far back as the nineteenth century, Dubai has resisted taking the direction of the other UAE monarchies. When the British came in and negotiated agreements with other UAE monarchies, Dubai established itself as a port of power and significance, creating a flourishing economy through fishing, pearl diving, and the crafting of gold. Dubai has since been a power in international trade, long before it established its first free-trade agreements in the 1980s.

Prior to the formation and establishment of the UAE constitution, the ruler of Dubai, Sheikh Rashid Al Maktoum, made the risky decision to borrow money from Kuwait in order to begin the modernization of Dubai. It paid off. A new, modern airport was built, and Port Rashid was expanded. In the 1980s, Sheikh Rashid increased hotel capacity, launched Emirates Airline, and increased the amount of tourism in the region.

In 1990, after Sheikh Rashid's death, his son, Sheikh Maktoum, then known as Sheikh Mohammed, took over and carried on his father's legacy, further developing Dubai into an even more desirable tourist destination and constructing the famous Burj Al Arab hotel. Sheikh Mohammed also expanded the Jebel Ali Free Zone, which was originally established by his father.

Aside from financial stability, Dubai—and the United Arab Emirates as a whole—has a tremendous amount of political stability. The people and even the foreign laborers give the state very little trouble. This is in large part thanks to the leadership of Sheikh Zayed bin Sultan Al-Nahyan, who was the founder and leader of the United Arab Emirates until his death in 2004, at which time there was a great outpouring of grief at his passing. Sheikh Zayed not only was the first president of the United Arab Emirates but also ensured that revenue from the oil industry benefited his people through infrastructure, health care, and education. This not only made the United Arab Emirates a desirable and safe place to live but also made it stable enough for Dubai to flourish and grow into the city it is today.

Dubai Today

The leaders of Dubai took their cue from the West, taking on projects that would help Dubai's economy thrive. While oil was one source of funds that gave them the jump start they needed, these days revenue from oil and gas make up only 7 percent of the total revenue in Dubai. Plus, the city will lose its oil reserves in twenty years. Sustained wealth has come from developing real estate that has drawn investors and tourists from around the world.

Dubai has become a very popular destination with tourists, primarily due to the unique experience it has to offer. It is one of the most expensive cities in the world, in which one can find the tallest building in the world, the Burj Khalifa, and one of the most expensive hotels in the world, the Burj Al Arab. The unique construction of buildings and real estate contributes more than 22 percent of the city's revenue, followed by trade at 16 percent and the financial-services industry at 11 percent. In addition, one of the largest shopping malls in the world is in Dubai, and the city attracts the rich because it is rich. The shopping experience is one of the best and most extravagant in the world.

However, Dubai has also become a high-tech hub, with its Internet City, which is a free zone similar to Jebel Ali, and its Media City, a free zone for the media presence in Dubai. Dubai is also a regional center of finance, attracting investors because of its liberal lending policies. State and private entities benefit equally from banks' lending capital. The Dubai International Financial Center is the city's financial free zone, a stable platform from which to do business.

Opportunities in Dubai

With all of the opportunity and potential to be tapped into in Dubai, there is little wonder why people turn to the city as a means of creating wealth. The reputation of the city has spread far and wide. In 2014, Dubai was named by *Forbes* as one of the world's most influential cities, beating out metropolises such as Beijing, Sydney, Los Angeles, San Francisco, and Toronto. Dubai was also named the Middle East City of the Future in 2013 by *fDI Magazine*, the third consecutive time the city was given the honor.

One of the most critical factors in determining which cities rank as *fDI Magazine*'s Middle East City of the Future is the ability of the city to offer a business environment that is accessible, the number of days to get a business start-up off the ground, corporate tax, and the number of jobs foreign investment creates within the city. With this business mentality and infrastructure well established in Dubai, it's no wonder people flock to the city to take advantage of the opportunity to become wealthy.

So when it comes down to it, in what ways are people able to take advantage of what Dubai has to offer and become wealthy? The key is to invest in the industries that are flourishing in Dubai. The city is to continuously create new ways to bring in money, especially in view of the fact that there are plans to host Expo 2020 and create underwater hotels and even full-scale replicas of the Eiffel Tower and Taj Mahal. But really, when it comes to getting rich in Dubai, it's not just about the investment opportunities but about the other supports in place to help people reap the financial benefits of the city:

- There is no income tax. None. Plus, most employers in Dubai pay their employees' housing fees for them.
- The gas is incredibly cheap—cheaper than water.
- They are serious about safety in the city of Dubai. There is a very low crime rate, which means insurance premiums are lower, and your money is safer.
- The local population provides inexpensive labor, which is ideal for people wanting to hire help for their businesses or servants to work in their homes.

Obstacles and Myths about Getting Rich in Dubai

Of course, nothing is perfect, and when in Dubai, there are some things that can work against you when it comes to personal finances. These are things that it would be wise to keep in mind if you are not from Dubai and not in the know:

- Rent is expensive.
- Public services, little bit expensive comparing it with other emirates.

- Vat " value added tax" to be introduced to UAE in 2018.

Aside from these, be prepared for incredibly hot weather, twenty degrees Celsius in the depths of winter and over fifty degrees Celsius at the height of summer.

Reflection

If you already live in Dubai, the United Arab Emirates, or the Middle East, you are familiar with the culture and climate of Dubai. If not, then you should go into it with some knowledge and an idea of what you want when you get there. Take the time to get to know Dubai more intimately—where you might live, in what you might like to invest, and avenues for bringing in a stream of income that will make your dreams come true. You can write down your thoughts and findings and keep these at the forefront of your mind as you continue reading.

The next chapter will focus on why people fail to find wealth and riches in Dubai, despite their best efforts. Then the rest of the book will focus on my philosophy for success so that you can achieve all the wealth and riches you desire *and* deserve.

Chapter 2: Why People Get in Their Own Way

We are dying from overthinking. We are slowly killing ourselves by thinking about everything. Think. Think. Think. You can never trust the human mind anyway. It's a death trap.

—Anthony Hopkins

Here is the thing when it comes to success and becoming wealthy, whether you are seeking this success and wealth in Dubai or somewhere else. The majority of people don't achieve the level of success they desire. Why? Simply put, because they get in their own way. People stop themselves from becoming rich, even when living in a place like Dubai, which offers so much potential.

How do we get in our own way? How is it when we seem to want something so badly—and we know, at least on some level, that we are perfectly capable of accomplishing our goals—we go so far astray and fail to succeed? It comes down to one simple concept, one that is capable of weaseling its way into any and every aspect of our lives. We overthink things.

Yes, that is really it, in a nutshell. We get in our own way by overthinking things. We might think too much about what we should be doing and how we should be doing it rather than simply letting ourselves do what we have been trained to do. We overthink things when we question ourselves or the opportunities that present themselves, wondering if they are worth it, if we deserve it, or if it's even possible. Our thinking can really get in our way when we let it. Let's take a look at the ways in which our thinking stops us from achieving success and wealth.

Procrastination

Wealth is something you want badly enough to be reading this book. You have thought about it and thought about it some more. You have schemed and planned and determined how you will take Dubai by storm and make your fortune. Then you put it off. What is this all about? Procrastination. It is the act of voluntarily putting something off that we know we must do, and if we don't get it done, we will suffer the consequences. In psychological terms, procrastination is an inability to self-regulate. Although everyone procrastinates at least sometimes, some people are chronic procrastinators.

That brings us to the *why*. Why do people procrastinate, particularly when it is something that matters so much to them? There are a few different reasons, one or more of which might apply when it comes to pursuing wealth in Dubai. Let's take a look at them.

Insufficient Skills

In order to build wealth, people need to know what to do and how to do it. Understanding the world of business and investment requires a certain set of skills, skills you may or may not have. When people are uncertain about whether they have the right skills to make something happen, it is reasonable to expect that they will put it off, which is one of the main reasons so many people procrastinate.

When it comes to building wealth in a place such as Dubai, it is understandable that if you don't know where to begin, it can be difficult to get started. Perhaps you don't want to admit to other people in the business world that you are unsure of yourself or don't fully understand some of the processes and actions required to build wealth. This can easily happen when you are immersed in Dubai's culture, a place in which the people probably all appear to be very adept in business and seem to know precisely what they are doing at all times.

Solution: In this case, you can go to school to acquire the necessary skills. You can also get a job within a financial or investment institution or get a mentor, someone who can show you the ropes. There is no shame in admitting that you don't know everything and that you need help.

Insufficient Interest

If you are working toward getting rich in Dubai, the end goal certainly interests you. However, no matter what we want to do in life, there are always stages along the way and things we have to learn or do that we don't have any interest in whatsoever. Someone might have a passion to run an art-collecting business but finds the tedium of cataloguing the art or taking care of the finances of the business boring compared to searching for and acquiring the pieces and creating incredible art displays and shows.

Solution: Bite the bullet. There will come a time when you can hire someone to do the things you dislike or find boring. Until then, perhaps you can reward yourself after you complete a boring task or reach a goal related to an aspect of your business that you dislike.

Insufficient Motivation

Speaking of rewards, motivation is often a reason for procrastination. Yes, you are motivated by your end result. You sit there and imagine what it will be like when you have built up your wealth and have the kind of life in Dubai you want to live. But getting there requires a lot of hard work, sometimes doing things you don't want to do. It's difficult to start doing something that you don't feel motivated to do, and it is also difficult to accomplish something when your attitude is one that gets in the way of motivation.

Solution: It is common for people to think they need to feel motivated to start a task, but in fact, the opposite is true. It is better to start the task first, and as you work through the task, the motivation will come. It is also important to get rid of any attitude or stinking thinking that requires something to be interesting to be motivating. Perhaps it is time to accept that not every aspect of reaching your dream will be interesting or fun; but it is all worthwhile.

Fear of Failure

We have all heard this one before, that a fear of failure can hold us back. Well, it's true. A fear of trying and not accomplishing what we set out to do can be a reason for procrastination. What if you put everything you have into your pursuit of wealth in Dubai and lose it all because you don't succeed?

Sometimes people think it's better to fail as a result of not trying hard enough rather than failing after having given it their all. If we put off what needs to be done, we are protecting ourselves from the inevitable failure we perceive will occur. Perfectionism has a hand in this fear, creating an expectation to meet standards set by you, your family, or someone else.

Solution: In order to overcome the fear of failure, it is important to recognize that you may have set unrealistic standards. Whatever the standard is in terms of your ultimate goal, if you believe it is real in the long run, then breaking that goal down into smaller, more manageable pieces that are easier to achieve is a better approach. Then you are only going after that one smaller goal. If the larger goal or standard isn't realistic, then redefine it—no matter who set it in the first place.

Fear of Success

Yes, some people actually fear success. Perhaps they fear they won't know how to repeat their performance, the one that brought them to success in the first place. Perhaps they fear the attention they will receive if they succeed. Some people even fear success because they wouldn't know what to do with it, or they feel they don't really deserve it, which is an issue of self-esteem and self-worth.

Solution: You must understand that no matter what level of success you reach or don't reach, you are good enough. No matter what standards are set and who set them, you can reach them with confidence and enjoy each step. What comes next, the next set of expectations, is in no way related to what you have already accomplished.

The Need to Resist/Rebel

Chances are, if you are looking to achieve wealth and riches in Dubai, this is your own set of goals and expectations. There is no need to resist or rebel against yourself. But perhaps there is someone with whom you are dealing who has done something to upset you, made demands you don't like, or set expectations of how you will reach your goal. You might procrastinate in taking a step toward your goal of creating wealth simply to rebel against that person.

Solution: Just remember that if you are resisting or rebelling against someone and it is causing you to procrastinate, you are allowing that person to have power over you. Ultimately, you are the one in control and calling the shots. You don't need to react to others; you need to follow your own path and make your own decisions.

Not Taking Advantage of Opportunity

Opportunity is defined by *Merriam-Webster* as "a favorable juncture of circumstances" or "a good chance for advancement or progress." If opportunity is so favorable and offers a chance to progress or advance in life, then why on earth would anyone pass up an opportunity that comes his or her way? Thomas Edison once said, "Opportunity is missed by most people because it is dressed in overalls and looks like work." This is indeed true in many circumstances. Whether you pass up a promotion at work, the chance to participate in a special project at the office, a blind date with someone your coworker swears is a great person, or the chance to go bungee jumping, these are all opportunities that would allow you to experience something new and exciting, something that could change your life forever.

A great example of the potential consequences of passing up an opportunity is when students pass up the opportunity to take a specific course in high school or college. They don't think it is something they will need, but as they carry on in their education, they might come to a point where a certain educational or career path is of interest to them, an educational or career path that required the course they didn't take. In other words, missed opportunities result in closed doors.

Let's consider an example that is more closely related to your desire to get rich in Dubai. Perhaps there is a chance to invest in a new business or commodity, and you pass it up, not having done your homework or thinking it won't amount to anything. Perhaps there is an opportunity that offers a fantastic return but requires an investment that is more than the funds you have available. In this instance, you could get a loan (borrowing may be justified in this instance), but you don't wish to go into debt. You pass up the opportunity, one that would have resulted in a return on investment that far exceeds any interest you might have paid on your loan.

Solution: The importance of taking opportunities that come your way is paramount to your success. *Any* given opportunity in business and in life has the potential to teach you new skills and information, help you meet new people who could be of help in reaching your financial and business goals, and help spark new ideas that could provide further opportunity. So if opportunity comes your way, it is advised that you do the following:

- Consider it. Don't just say no off the cuff. Take the time to consider the opportunity and what it could mean for you. Do some research and find out if the opportunity is one that has a high chance of benefiting you in the short or long term. This could be financial benefit, the benefit of knowledge and information, or the benefit of new professional contacts.
- Reflect. Take the time to look back and see if there are any opportunities you didn't take. Consider why you turned them down and what might have been if you had taken them. This can help you determine whether you have a pattern of missed opportunities and if there is some aspect of your behavior you need to work on.
- Allow yourself to take some risk. Obviously you don't want to break the bank or sink yourself so low you will never succeed. You don't want to fall for a scam. However, that doesn't mean that some level of risk isn't worth it. In fact, you can't achieve anything in life without a little risk. As part of your research and homework, conduct a risk assessment to see if the opportunity is right for you.
- Stay positive. When you are staring a new opportunity in the face, be positive at all times. A positive attitude will help you overcome any setbacks that arise, offer you more opportunities, and allow you to recognize them when they come along.

Complaining

Complaining has the potential to be the most useless, unconstructive thing a person can do. It is so easy to complain about what isn't going well in life, what you don't have in life, and whose fault it is. Nevertheless, everyone needs to complain at one time or another. It can be a way to

- vent when things seem to be going wrong;
- find motivation;
- get things done or resolve an unacceptable situation;
- find a solution to a problem; and
- help us gain another perspective on a situation.

However, complaining can also become a very nasty habit, and it can hold us back from the amazing things we can accomplish, because we are so focused on the negative that we can't see what is positive or what great opportunities are right in front of us.

Complaining can also do more than turn us down the path of missed opportunity. Research has shown that people who complain on a regular basis are less healthy, have less satisfying relationships that last for less time than those of their positive counterparts, and tend to do worse in their jobs or careers. Complaining also creates a negative atmosphere in which others do not want to be because it is draining to be around someone who is frequently or constantly negative.

This brings up a good question. If complaining is so horribly bad for us and our lives, why do people do it? As mentioned above, complaining can easily become a habit, and it is a way to focus on the negative in life, but complaining also offers a way

- for people to connect in conversation, since complaining tends to bring people together;
- for people to validate what they believe or feel;
- to put responsibility onto others; and
- to put off taking action.

Solution: How can a person escape the habit of complaining? Fortunately, when a person is open to considering that he or she may have a problem with complaining, there are steps he or she can take to turn things around. Consider the following steps to a more positive life:

1. Be aware. The very first thing you need to do is learn to become aware of when you are complaining. Try to observe everything you say for the next twenty-four hours and catch yourself when you start to complain. Learn to determine when it is happening and what might trigger it.
2. Once you are aware of your negative complaints, you can trace these to the thoughts you are having. You need to take responsibility for those thoughts because you are the one who created them. When you have the ability to link your complaints to your thoughts, you can then ask yourself what the intention of complaining about each particular thought is.
3. After you have done this, you can consider what you actually want and determine whether or not the complaint is helping you achieve that. The key here is to be clear about what you want and, conversely, what you don't want.
4. Because you have been able to isolate what you really want, you can then find ways to replace the negative thoughts and complaints with something positive. If you are complaining that you keep getting passed over for a promotion at work and you decide that what you really want is recognition and the chance to move up in the company, you can decide how to go about achieving that, which might begin with speaking with your supervisor and asking directly why you haven't been promoted and what you can do to increase your chances of getting a promotion.

Remember that complaining generally doesn't accomplish anything. Simply put, if you are complaining about something that cannot be changed, then it's really just a waste of breath, other than perhaps allowing you to vent a little. If you are complaining about something that can be changed, then complaining won't accomplish that. Instead, channel that energy and take whatever action you can to make that change become a reality.

Reflection

Take some time to determine whether you are affected by any of the above ways of thinking that keep people from achieving success—procrastination, passing opportunity by, and complaining. In the discussion of each of these issues, there is a solution provided for how to make changes in your life so that you can stop following those patterns. For each way of thinking in which you engage, choose a situation in your life and use the suggested solution to see if you can find another, better way to deal with that real-life situation.

Now that you have a solid concept of why people do not succeed in reaching their goals and how you can address these specific situations, it is time to move on to my philosophy and formula for success. We will begin with a general introduction to the philosophy and formula and follow that up with a thorough explanation of each aspect of the formula. When put together, the formula will give you the mental and emotional ability to create any life you desire. Let's get started.

Chapter 3: My Philosophy for Getting Rich

Problems or successes, they all are the results of our own actions. Karma. The philosophy of action is that no one else is the giver of peace or happiness. One's own karma, one's own actions are responsible to come to bring either happiness or success or whatever.

—Maharishi Mahesh Yogi

Whenever you ask people how to get rich, they will generally throw financial facts at you. You will be told that you need to work hard to earn enough money to invest. Put in your hours and you will have the money to show for it, and then get your money working for you by investing in start-up companies, the stock market, or real estate, and avoid making senseless purchases. Financial gurus will discuss the best ways to invest, the skills you need to play the financial game, and how important it is to save money and stay out of debt.

OK, the first thing to be said here is that these are valid points, all of them. To get rich, you do need to work hard and not give up. All of this concrete action matters, but if you don't have the right frame of mind, if your perspective is clouded, the action will be for naught. You might—maybe—be lucky enough to get rich, but if you do, you probably won't be happy.

Happiness Matters

This is such a sticky topic. Can money buy you happiness? No. Well, mostly no. I say mostly because if you don't have enough money to buy the necessities of life, then you won't be happy. If you aren't able to meet your family's basic needs, then you won't be happy. If you are struggling to pay your rent or mortgage each month, don't have enough money to get the food you need, or are falling behind in paying your bills, you aren't going to be happy. In fact, you'll be downright miserable and stressed. Nothing else will matter. It's that simple.

If you wonder whether happiness matters, it does—at least according to a survey conducted by Action for Happiness. They polled adults in the United Kingdom, and 87 percent of the respondents said they would prefer to live in a happy country than a rich country. These people answered as if happiness and money are not mutually exclusive, yet people generally behave as if they are. So why doesn't money buy happiness? Here are three reasons that may surprise you:

It's all relative: People compare themselves to whoever is around them. Having a significantly high income isn't necessarily important, provided we are earning more than the people around us. The problem with this is that as we earn more money, we are more likely to surround ourselves with people who earn more money. We will move into a wealthier neighborhood and shop at pricier stores. Before long, we are once again earning less than the people around us and striving for more to get ahead of them.

More things do not mean happier people: People who have more money tend to buy more things. We have this desire to buy cars, clothes, jewelry, fancy furniture, and anything else we can imagine, but any happiness we have when we buy these things is fleeting. In fact, it has been proved that the more materialistic people are, the unhappier they are and the more likely they are to be depressed, narcissistic, and paranoid.

The millennial generation that is now taking over the workforce has figured this out, and *Forbes* reports that this generation is looking for happiness. They feel that happiness is more important than money. They are loyal to the job rather than their employer, and they are concerned with having a good work-life balance. *Forbes* also found that millennials would rather buy experiences over material possessions. They referred to a study conducted by Harris and sponsored by Eventbrite. The results of the study showed that millennials desire time spent with loved ones and experiences that create memories, allow for bonding, and provide a sense of community. The study says, "For this group, happiness isn't as focused on possessions or career status. Living a meaningful, happy life is about creating, sharing and capturing memories earned through experiences that span the spectrum of life's opportunities."

This brings us to the third reason money doesn't buy happiness:

When people get rich, they don't pursue enjoyable activities. When people get rich, they don't tend to change the way they live. They worked hard to earn money, and they just keep on working hard. As they keep working as hard as ever, they get more and more stressed. This breeds a different kind of unhappiness, not the kind brought about from not having enough money but the kind of unhappiness that comes from working all the time to earn more and more money at the expense of actually living.

What's the point of working eighty-hour weeks to earn six figures? It's not like you'll have the time to enjoy any of the money you've made. That money might buy you nice things; it will even buy you experiences, which are what really matter, but you have no time to experience anything. You're working all the time.

Obviously, there is something to be said about how you earn your money in terms of technique. Working longer hours isn't the answer; getting your money working for you is. However, there is more to it than that.

It's Not What You Do

I mentioned above that financial skills matter, and it's true that they do, but at the same time, they are not everything. In fact, these skills alone won't guarantee success. Think about it. How many people have gone to good schools? How many people have graduated with good grades? How many people have the skills to know how to invest their money? Get into real estate? Read the markets? The answer: millions and millions of people. Yet not all of these people are truly wealthy. Sure, they might live comfortably enough that they have a decent house, and maybe they can take their families on vacation once a year, but they aren't truly wealthy. They are the middle class.

This tells us that having the skills to know what to do is simply not enough to be truly successful and wealthy. So what is it that creates success? It's the philosophy behind what you do. It's all a mind game. In order to find true wealth, you need to have the right mind-set. This mind-set includes the following general concepts, all of which are covered in the remaining chapters of this book:

- See yourself being wealthy and successful. Your mind is a brilliant thing, far more than you probably realize. It will do more than simply calculate numbers for you.
- Find out what truly motivates you. Everyone has the same basic motivators. Everyone needs to eat and have clothing and a place to live. We all also need to feel as though we fit in and, beyond that, to develop ourselves, but how each of us does these things is an individual journey that we choose. Determining what motivates you is critical to your success because you will use that, rely on it, and let it propel you forward even when you feel like quitting.
- Change the way you think. Yes, there are certain circumstances in your life, but these do not dictate your level of success. Instead, success is determined by what you do with these circumstances or despite them. The key is to change your frame of mind, to go beyond what life has dealt you, and forge your way ahead.
- Use those negative emotions. There will be times when you are down; maybe now is one of those times. But you have a choice. You can wallow in those defeating emotions, or you can take the energy from those and channel them into creating the life you want. It's all about attitude.
- Take action. Sometimes we are simply paralyzed, stuck in inaction, and not sure how to get moving to accomplish what we want to accomplish. People have a wonderful talent for thinking or talking something to death and never actually *doing* anything. Don't get stuck going down this path. There is always something you can do to improve your situation and move in the right direction, so *do* it.
- Check in with yourself. It is important that you check in with yourself along this journey to wealth and success to see where you are in terms of reaching your goals. Checking in will allow you to take stock and alter your course if you find you are getting off track or if you misjudged the direction in which you need to go. These self-assessments are critical to success.

Reflection

Take some time to consider whether any of the topics in the list above resonate with you. Are there any that you already do? Are there any that you know you don't do but wish you did? Is there something you think you struggle with? As we move into the following chapters, keep these thoughts in mind. You will perhaps develop a better understanding of yourself and what is holding you back from true success and wealth as you read on.

With this seed firmly planted in your mind, we will now move on to discussing each of the above points in the following chapters. Take it all in, and don't dismiss anything out of hand. There may be some good things in this guide that you never realized before and that can help you turn your life around for the better.

Chapter 4: You Are Only Limited by Your Imagination

The world of reality has its limits; the world of imagination is boundless.

—Jean-Jacques Rousseau

In this chapter, we are going to discuss the importance of imagination. Imagination is not given the credit it really deserves. When most people think of imagination, they think of the arts. They think of paintings and sculptures and writing and other forms of art. But imagination is responsible for so much more than just art.

When thinking of the things we imagine, it is easy to consider these things as fanciful—as things that don't really exist. But think about this. Before the telephone was invented, it was just something that existed in the imagination of Alexander Graham Bell. Before the first airplane was built, it was just an idea that existed in the imaginations of Orville and Wilbur Wright. Before the Empire State Building was erected, it was just a blueprint in the imagination of William F. Lamb.

Do you see where I'm going with this? Every single thing that you see around you, everything you can touch, everything you use in your daily life, and everything everywhere was first an idea in someone's mind. Someone imagined that it could exist, *but they didn't stop there*. Once they imagined it, they *knew* it would exist, and they made that imagination become reality.

This is one way that imagination is instrumental in the creation of reality. But the imagination and the mind can do so much more. The mind can not only imagine what you want to become reality, the idea or concept you have created, but also imagine you achieving your goals. The act of visualization is very powerful and is something that is a necessity to help you attain the wealth you desire. Since we have two different aspects of imagination, let's look at each of them independently.

What Imagination Is

The first thing to consider is what imagination is. Do you know what it is? Perhaps yes or perhaps no. Essentially, imagination is a person's ability to see or experience something in his or her mind. This can come in the form of images, sounds, smells, and other sensations. It is something that does not physically exist, is not in the person's presence, or is from the past. The first thing you absolutely must know is that everyone has the ability to imagine. However, some people have an easier time with it than others.

Just think about children. Have you ever seen a child who can't imagine—who can't create things in his or her mind that have no real bearing on reality? In some cases, they create their own reality. Unfortunately, this ability is not fostered as children grow up. We have to leave that childlike imagination behind. Our creativity and imagination are crushed by what is considered more important. How sad this is.

The greatest and most successful people are the ones who don't lose their imagination but take that imagination into whatever they do in life. These are the people who invent telephones and airplanes. These are the people who discover the laws of physics, become top athletes, and become truly wealthy, the top businesspeople in the world. It is not just the artists, writers, actors, and singers who enjoy the benefits of imagination; it's everyone who is able to tap into his or her imagination and let it soar.

So, let's get something straight right now—daydreaming is a *good* thing. It is a good thing to let your mind wander because it taps into your creativity. Once you get used to allowing your mind to do this, your imagination will start to focus on the things in your life and will begin to sort things out for you, coming up with solutions to problems and ways to make life better. This is what you want working for you. Let's see how your imagination can help.

From Concept to Reality

What is reality? No, we are not going to get into a discussion of reality like the concept in the movie *The Matrix* or the game Mortal Kombat, but it is important to understand that our reality is how we imagine it.

Reality is linked with thought and imagination. Consider the negative people you know. There is bound to be at least one negative person in your life, someone who complains about everything, never takes responsibility for his or her own life, and always sees the worst in every situation. Take a good, long look at the life of this person. Is it a good life? A happy life? I would wager a guess that it isn't. It is unlikely that this person is living the life he or she truly wants to be living.

Your whole life, your whole reality, starts in your mind. You create your life there first. Henry Ford knew the power of thought. He said, "Whether you believe you can do a thing or not, you are right."

In other words, if you doubt or don't think something is attainable, then it won't be, but if you think it is attainable, it is. You see, it works like this. If you think you can't do something or that something isn't possible, then you aren't even going to bother trying. You will not take any action toward making it happen because, well, why would you? There isn't any point in trying if it isn't possible, right? But that is exactly why it isn't possible, because you don't bother trying. And you don't bother trying because you don't think it's possible.

What about the other side of the coin? What about when you think something is possible—when you think you can accomplish or do something? If you think it is possible, you will think about that thing actually happening and about what life would be like with it as reality. Then you will do the things you need to do to make it a reality. You will take the steps necessary to make it happen because—why not? You can do it, and it is possible, so you should make it happen.

When individuals want something badly enough and believe it can happen, they will do what they need to do to achieve their goals, but they have to get out of their own way. Sometimes we get discouraged and doubt whether we really can achieve our goals in life. There are also many people who don't believe they deserve good things in their lives. Many people ruin themselves because of low self-esteem. These people don't think they will be happy until they have what they want, they feel shame on an ongoing basis, and they doubt themselves and feel like imposters.

The first thing you absolutely have to do is believe in yourself. You are worthy of success and wealth. That's it. Period. Repeat this phrase to yourself over and over again every day, even if you don't think you need to. Repeat it to yourself even if you think you are worthy of success and wealth.

"I am worthy of success and wealth. I deserve success and wealth."

Say it when you get up, say it throughout the day, and say it when you go to bed. It sounds like you're trying to convince yourself that you are worthy, and guess what? You are! And it will work if you tell yourself this regularly. If you do this, it will become reality.

But you also need to get your imagination involved in the process because what you imagine will become your reality. With that in mind, we are now going to talk about the power of visualization.

The Power of Visualization

Have you ever heard of visualization? I am guessing you probably have, and maybe you have even tried it before. Visualization is a very powerful thing. Visualization makes use of your imagination to make things happen in your life. How? Well, here's the funny thing. Did you know your brain cannot tell the difference between something that is imagined and something that is real? Here is a scenario that you can consider.

You love your morning newspaper. Every day your morning routine is to get up, make the coffee, and collect the morning newspaper from the front door. But one day, the paper isn't there. You look over at your neighbor, and he is going into his house with a newspaper in hand. You wonder about that because he never did subscribe to newspaper delivery, but you go in and call the newspaper office to ask them to redeliver it. For a whole week, you don't get your newspaper, and you have seen your neighbor with a paper every morning. Your anger has been growing all week. Your neighbor is stealing your newspaper—the paper that you pay your hard-earned money for that rounds out your morning routine.

One day, you decide you are going to go confront your neighbor. After all, enough is enough. You see your neighbor on his front porch, and you start down your front steps. That's when you notice a bunch of newspapers lying on the ground between your porch and the hedge in front of it. You reach down and pick them up, and there are all the papers you have been missing all week.

You call the newspaper office and find out there has been a new delivery person who isn't taking much care when he throws your newspaper onto your front step. He has been missing and not bothering to check to make sure it lands properly. The problem is taken care of, but you still feel angry toward your neighbor. Then he comes over to ask if he can borrow your car because his is broken. All of the anger you have been building up the whole week is right there, and it's all you can do to be nice and say yes to his request.

Now think about this. Your neighbor never actually did anything wrong. It turns out he started subscribing to the newspaper a couple of weeks ago, but you didn't know. For a whole week, you have been getting angrier and angrier over a scenario that you created in your mind, but the feelings are very real. You really are angry, even though it isn't real.

That is the power of imagination and visualization.

Now, let's take a look at how this can help you achieve what you want. Let's say you have a garage that is packed full of all sorts of junk and things that have to be cleared out. These are things that have been collected over many years. You look at the mess in front of you, and you feel discouraged, not wanting to do the work.

But here is the problem. We all tend to think of the work involved, not the end result. When we think of all the work it will take, we feel awful about it. Just thinking about all that work makes us feels tired, grumpy, stressed out, and unhappy. Who would want to do anything when they feel that way?

But what if you changed your thinking? What if you actually visualized the finished product? What if you saw in your mind the cleaned-out garage? What if you visualized your car parked in the garage or room for the new boat you want to buy? That is an image that makes you feel happy, but more than that, you feel like you accomplished something, that you succeeded in achieving what you set out to do. That is the kind of feeling and emotion that spurs you on to action and gets you moving.

The key here is to visualize what you are striving for, to visualize the end result rather than the work it takes to get there. When you visualize the end result, you will feel the feelings of success and accomplishment that go along with it, and then you will take the action you need to take to actually achieve the reality.

This is how you can use your imagination to achieve your dreams and goals of being successful and wealthy. You need to visualize the end result, not all the work you have to do to get there. You need to know how to visualize and achieve. Remember, it isn't just about the skills and the opportunity. You have the skills, and Dubai is filled with nothing but opportunity. You need to actually imagine yourself in the life you want. You need to visualize it. Here are some ways to do that:

Avoid fantasizing. You need to keep your visualization at a level that will ensure you can succeed. What do I mean by this? If you visualize your complete end result and only that, you might not see the possible problems that might come up along the way. While it is good to keep your final destination in mind, you should also break up that journey into smaller goals and visualize the completion of each one as you go. This way, you will be more likely to see potential obstacles and devise ways to overcome them. Your feeling of success will build, and you will accomplish the overall goal.

Eliminate negative thoughts. Negative thoughts always want to creep in and crash the positive party you have going on inside your head. This cannot be allowed, ever. Whenever you catch yourself doubting yourself or thinking negatively, you need to squash those thoughts and move on. We will talk more in a later chapter about what to do when we have negativity running through us.

Meditate. You can meditate on your final destination and the smaller goals you have set up along the way. Take some time every day to sit quietly and visualize your success. See yourself as wealthy and living the lifestyle you want to live. See yourself with money, with investments, with the car and home you want. Go and sit in Palm Jumeirah for no other reason than to feel the environment. Put yourself there and then meditate on the next goal that you must reach to achieve that ultimate success. See yourself achieving that goal and being one step closer to your ultimate success. When you take the time to meditate on and visualize both the ultimate success and the next goal, you will keep the emotion of success alive and well and still be focused on the next step to get there. You can perhaps do one visualization meditation in the morning and another at night.

Create a visualization board. Again, you can do this for your ultimate success and the current goal you are working to achieve. Get some poster board. Then look for pictures (in magazines or on the Internet) of anything that to you symbolizes the success and wealth you want to create. These might be pictures of money, a nice home, vacations, a nice car, or something that represents the freedom that wealth will give you. Place this visualization board somewhere you will see it every day. Do the same for the goal you are currently working to achieve. You can change the short-term goal visualization board each time you hit a goal, but you will always have the main visualization board that represents your final goal.

Here I want to offer you a final word on visualization. Think of visualizing what you want to happen as a rehearsal or practice. You can visualize how you will accomplish something over and over in your mind. You can see what could go wrong, and you can fix it in your mind without any repercussions in the real world. You can rehearse the actions that will help you achieve your goals without having to worry about failure because it's all in your imagination. When you feel ready to take action for real, you will already feel confident and able to be successful.

Reflection

You probably already know what you want in terms of success. Chances are, it is to find your way to riches in Dubai. However, it can be anything at all. At this point, it is time to put your powerful imagination to work:

- *Each morning visualize yourself living the life you want. See yourself in the home you want. See yourself driving the car you want. See yourself vacationing where you want. Immerse yourself in this visualization, and let the emotions come to you.*
- *Set up a series of short-term goals to reach your ultimate goal of being rich. Take the time to write these goals down. Each night visualize the goal you are currently working on. See yourself achieving that goal. Imagine yourself doing what you need to do to get it done, and see yourself when you achieve the goal. As you achieve each goal in reality, move on to visualizing the next goal.*
- *Create a visualization board for your ultimate goal and the goal you are currently working on. While this might seem like a childish exercise, the act of creating this board* and *writing down your goals will help cement your goals and desires in your subconscious mind. Your subconscious mind will then ensure you act in the way you need to act to achieve those goals.*

Take the time to create some affirmations that really matter to you. Make sure these are words or short phrases that have meaning for you and will help inspire and motivate you toward the success you desire. Have these affirmations reflect your visualizations, and say them repeatedly throughout the day.

Imagination is truly a powerful thing. It will help you tap into your desire for success and what motivates you to achieve that success. But what is motivation? Does motivation really matter all that much? Isn't everyone motivated? Read on. In the next chapter, we will discuss what motivation really is and how to harness its power to work for you.

Chapter 5: Let Motivation and Inspiration Push You

Part 1: Motivation

Desire is the key to motivation, but it's determination and commitment to an unrelenting pursuit of your goal—a commitment to excellence—that will enable you to attain the success you seek.

—Mario Andretti

What is motivation? Have you ever really asked yourself that question? The *Merriam-Webster Dictionary* defines motivation as "the act or process of giving someone a reason for doing something." This reason is a need or desire. Therefore, motivation is a combination of needs and desires that push us to do what we need to do to successfully achieve our goals.

Now, we need to be clear on what constitutes need and what constitutes desire. These are different, and there are different levels of each. Needs are what we must have to live (literally) and be happy, functional people in the world. Desires are the things we want to enjoy life better. Sometimes what we need and want are the same thing, but often we have desires that have nothing to do with our core needs, or they are embellished versions of those needs. For example, we need clothing to live, but do we need a T-shirt that costs fifty dollars when a ten-dollar T-shirt will do? Let's take a look at how each of these, needs and desires, have an effect on our pursuit of financial success in attaining wealth in Dubai.

Needs as Motivators

Every single person on this planet has certain needs. These needs were mapped out by Abraham Maslow in the 1940s. Maslow discovered that each human being has the same needs and that there are some needs that are more important than others. The needs form a hierarchy in which a person will not strive to meet the needs of one level until the needs of the previous levels have been met. Maslow's hierarchy is as follows:

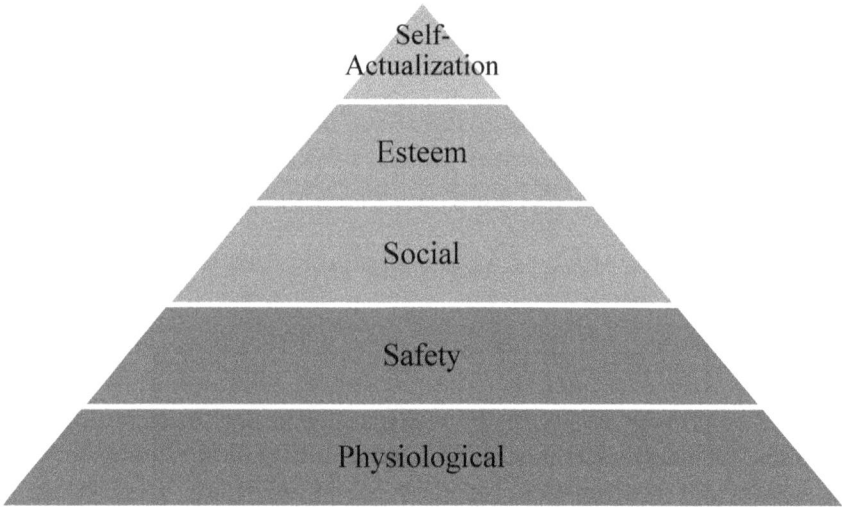

Starting from the base of the pyramid and moving up, the needs are as follows:

1. *Physiological needs.* These are the basic needs of life, such as water, food, air, and shelter.
2. *Safety needs.* These include anything needed to feel safe and protected. This is the need for security, which comes from law and order, stability, and limits.
3. *Social needs.* These are related to the need to belong and be loved and include the need for family, affection, and relationships.
4. *Esteem needs.* These involve feelings of self-worth and include responsibility, achievement, status, and reputation.
5. *Self-actualization needs.* These revolve around personal growth and fulfillment.

By the 1960s, Maslow's hierarchy of needs was revised to include three additional levels. The hierarchy now looks like this:

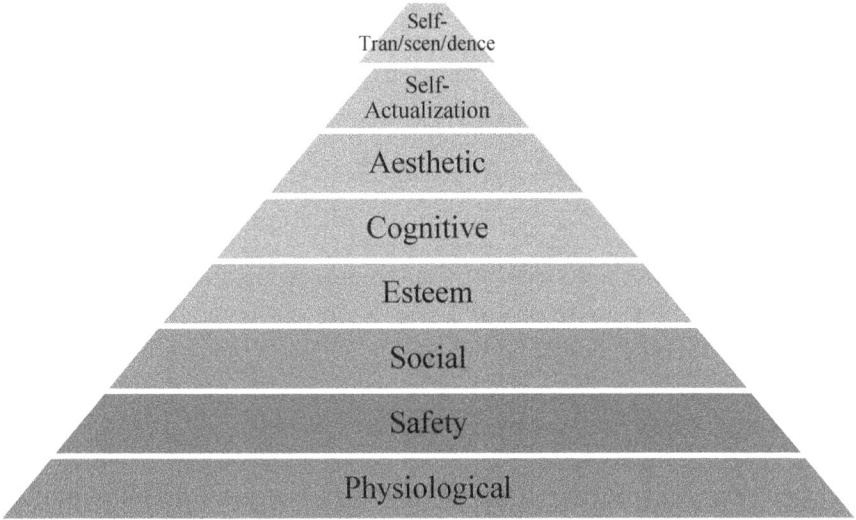

The additional levels of the hierarchy include:

- *Cognitive needs.* These needs relate to gathering knowledge with the goal of finding meaning and understanding in life.
- *Aesthetic needs.* These needs relate to self-expression in a manner that is pleasing, which can take the form of changing the environment in which we live, work, and play. The goal is to find beauty and balance.
- *Self-transcendence needs.* These relate to having goals that exist outside of ourselves, that go beyond our own personal basic needs. Helping others is included in this level of the hierarchy.

These needs fall into two broad categories:

Deficiency Needs	Growth Needs
Physiological	Cognitive
Safety	Aesthetic
Social	Self-actualization
Esteem	Self-transcendence

You may be wondering what these needs have to do with getting rich in Dubai. I'll explain it to you. Every person on the planet pursues these needs in order, from the bottom to the top, and there are no exceptions. These needs drive you just as much as they drive everyone else.

Chances are, if you have no money and no stability to provide the basics of food and a roof over your head, you won't be terribly concerned with generating large amounts of wealth. You will get whatever job you can find to bring in enough money to cover these basics. I assume you are past this point and that you have the financial ability to provide the basic necessities of life for you and your family.

You also want to feel safe and secure. Fortunately, in Dubai that is easy to do since, as mentioned in chapter 1, Dubai has minimal to no crime. You want to feel that you belong, that you have people who love you and accept you as one of theirs. Finally, you want to feel that you are worthy. This last one is somewhat interesting because people often think they become worthy only when they have achieved wealth or whatever goal they set out for themselves. Yet if they don't feel worthy before they achieve their goals, then how do they manage to achieve them? The key is to achieve a feeling of self-worth before you can truly achieve your goal of becoming wealthy. You are worth it before it happens.

These last two needs also bring up the point of accountability, which is something that you can use to help motivate you. Because you want to fit in, be recognized by your friends, and look good in the eyes of others, you will want to be accountable for your actions and what you commit to doing. If you say you are going to make something happen, then you will want to follow through and be successful. You don't want to look like a failure, and you don't want to damage your integrity. This is fabulous motivation.

So what if you have all of the deficiency needs met? Let's look at an example that may make this clearer. If you don't have the money to buy food and pay for a place to live, then your only concern is about getting a job to pay for these things. Nothing else matters. If you have these basics and you don't have companionship or love in your life, then you will look for a mate, someone to share your life with. But what if you have good employment and a comfortable home, and you can buy food and pay your bills? What if you also have a loving spouse and family? What if you feel safe and secure and loved and even worthy of all that you have in your life?

There are many people who have these things, and yet they still feel that something is missing in their lives. This is because their deficiency needs have been met, and they can and must now move on to the higher needs in Maslow's hierarchy—the growth needs, which are the cognitive, aesthetic, self-actualization, and self-transcendence needs.

These needs of humanity are critical when it comes to achieving wealth in Dubai or any of your other higher goals. If any of the above levels of the hierarchy have not been met, then get those in order before moving on to creating the wealth you want. Why? Because it takes time to create wealth, and you can't wait for that while your family is starving. You can't take your money and invest it and wait for a return on that investment when you and your family have nowhere to live. Get your basics in order, and then move on to building your wealth. This is still the beginning of the climb to wealth in Dubai; you just may be starting further down the ladder than someone else. Each person's starting point is unique and personal. Despite this, you can still end up on top.

Desires as Motivators

Desires are linked to our needs. It's like we have a need, but we don't want just the basics; we want to embellish that need far beyond what we need for survival. For instance, we need shelter, but does a family of four really *need* a house that is 2,678 square feet? This is the average size of a new house built today, but in the 1980s, the average was 1,700 square feet. My point is that we *need* a house, but we don't need it to be that big. Having a big house is a want.

The same can be said for a car. Some would even argue that a car is not really a need, which is likely true for people who live in urban centers where there is mass transportation. They can walk and bike to get where they are going. Right there it is easy to say a car is a want.

But let's say for the sake of argument that it is a need. Would a simple Ford Focus be enough, or does it have to be a Mercedes Benz G-63?

When it comes to clothing, we need clothes, but we can get regular clothes from the local department store. That's all we need. Yet people work hard to buy brand-name clothing such as Prada and Louis Vuitton.

Professor Emeritus Steven Reiss of Ohio State University conducted a study of six thousand people in 2000, and the result was his theory of motivation. This theory consists of the sixteen basic desires that motivate all human beings. These desires are

- acceptance;
- curiosity;
- eating;
- family;
- honor;
- idealism;
- independence;
- order;
- physical activity;
- power;
- romance;
- saving;
- social contact;
- social status;
- tranquility; and
- vengeance.

But when you look at these desires closely, it is easy to see that each one of the above desires can fit nicely into one of the levels of Maslow's hierarchy. These are really needs rather than desires.

So what are desires? In a nutshell, we take our needs and embellish them to the point where they become desires, like the big house and fancy clothes. But we also create desires that are completely independent of our needs. We don't need a yacht. We don't need to go to London every year. We don't need to wear a Rolex watch or have that weekend getaway in Paris. We don't need that cottage by the lake.

In terms of economics, a need is something that we must have to survive, and a want is something that is a step up from this—something a person desires for the sake of having that thing. Now, I'm not saying that having desires beyond the basics is wrong. They certainly drive and motivate us, even if the motivation and drive are not as strong as those born of our needs. However, we do need to find a balance in life between need and desire and learn what motivates us the most, particularly when we have met all of our deficiency needs.

When we are looking at our motivation to achieve our goal of getting rich in Dubai, we need to take a close look at our needs and desires. Chances are, your basic needs have been met. If any haven't, then you will be inclined to work on those first. But you can also make a list of your desires—the things you want above and beyond what you need to live. These desires will drive your behavior beyond what your needs are able to provide; they will drive you to extreme wealth. Let's take a look at how you can increase your motivation.

How to Increase Your Motivation

Now that you have a solid idea of what motivation is, where it comes from, and what drives it, it is worth considering how to increase that drive. How do you make your motivation even stronger? After all, we need to rely on what motivates us to keep us moving forward; otherwise, we will fail and quit. Let's take a look at how to strengthen your motivation.

Set Goals

The idea of setting goals is by no means a new concept. In fact, it's been around for a long time. Why? Because it works! Setting goals in the right way is important when it comes to reaching your dreams. What is the right way? You need to set SMART goals. Let's take a look at what SMART goals are.

Specific: Your goal has to be very specific. You cannot simply say, "I want to get rich." You have to make use of the six *W*s:

- Who: Who must be involved for you to reach your goal?
- What: What specifically do you want? Specify the number of dirhams you want.
- Where: Is there a specific place where you need to make this happen? Where in the United Arab Emirates? A specific company or investment location?
- When: When do you want to accomplish your goal? Do you want that specific number of dirhams within six months or a year?
- Which: Are there any constraints on reaching your goal or any requirements you need to meet in order to attain your goal?
- Why: Why exactly do you want to reach this goal? What is the benefit or purpose behind it?

Measurable: Your goal must have a set of criteria by which you can measure your progress. This means you have a specific end point in mind. If you are looking to get rich, then you need to determine what that means for you. Ask yourself how much, how many, and when. Do you want to have a million dirhams in a year's time? Break this large goal into smaller milestones that you can use to measure your progress and keep you on track.

Attainable: You must be capable of attaining your goal. By this, I mean that you need to have the right attitude, abilities, skills, and financial capacity to accomplish what you set out to do. This goes back to those skills we talked about earlier. They may only be one piece of the puzzle, but they are an important piece. Do you have the money to start investing? If not, then you need that first. If you are missing any of the things you need to accomplish your goal, you will become aware of these deficiencies and work to acquire these first.

Realistic: Something is realistic if it is something you are willing and able to work toward achieving. You need both willingness and ability. You might be willing to make 10 million dirhams in a year's time, but are you able to? Chances are, the answer is no. Set a goal that is worth striving for and set it high, but make sure it is something that you can realistically attain. What you decide on is up to you, but think about it carefully before you settle on your goal.

Timely: This is important. You can't watch a football match for two days nonstop. It would be boring. Above, I referred to doing something in a certain amount of time, and this is critical to your success. Not only do you need to know what you want, but you have to set a date, a concrete date, by which you want to achieve that goal. It isn't enough to say you want to get rich, and it isn't even enough to say you want to build your wealth to a million dirhams. If you don't assign a specific date to that number, then all you have is a someday, and somedays never come.

There are a couple more important points to know about setting SMART goals. First, your goals are not carved in stone. There will be times when you have to change a date by which you reach a milestone or change the milestone itself. If you have a road map and something comes up in life, such as an illness or injury that sets you back, you can reset the milestone and date to accommodate. Just remember that there will always be bumps in the road.

The second thing to know when it comes to setting goals is to write them down. You must write down your goals in detail. This is important because the act of writing down your goals helps instill these goals into your subconscious mind. Once you have cemented your goals into your subconscious, your subconscious will automatically steer you toward doing the things you need to do to achieve those goals.

Socialize with the Right People

If you want to be rich, then you need to surround yourself with and associate with rich people. Bring people into your life who are high achievers, those who are pursuing the same goals as you or who have achieved those goals already. Seeing how these people live and where they are in their journeys toward wealth will motivate you to carry on.

Celebrate Your Successes

When you hit a milestone and achieve success, celebrate. Recognize your accomplishments; you deserve to have some recognition. Recognizing and celebrating your accomplishments will help motivate you to the next milestone of your goal and help you keep moving forward because you can see that success is possible, and you can see that you are capable of doing what you set out to do.

Reflection

Take some time to write down your motivations. First, consider Maslow's hierarchy. Are there any needs from that that are motivating you to achieve wealth and success? Where do you feel you are on the hierarchy? Write down the needs that are motivating you. Next, consider your desires. Give it some thorough thought, and write down the desires that are motivating you to pursue your goal of becoming wealthy. Keep these lists to refer to later on, whenever you need to remind yourself why you are doing what you are doing.

Part 2: Inspiration

True inspiration overrides all fears. When you are inspired, you enter a trance state and can accomplish things that you may never have felt capable of doing.

—Bernie Siegel

We have talked extensively about motivation, and now it is time to discuss inspiration. How is motivation different from inspiration? Motivation is an external factor that drives you to accomplish things and reach your goals. Motivation can sometimes be painful, and sometimes you can feel like giving up despite your motivations. Inspiration is very different because it is a drive that comes from within. It's passion. It's something that you can't buy or attain. It is soul deep and propels you forward, unlike motivation, which is more of a forceful push to get things done. Inspiration can save you during those times when motivation just doesn't seem like enough to keep you moving forward.

Now that you know what inspiration is and how it differs from motivation, what is your inspiration? Do you have inspiration? Do you even know? Would you know inspiration if it walked up and smacked you in the face? Inspiration is about what you love, what you enjoy, what has touched your soul in a way no material item can. To find inspiration, you need to step outside yourself. Here are ways to find inspiration on your journey toward wealth.

Let Others Inspire You

One of the most common ways people are inspired is by learning the stories of other people. In particular, these are stories of ordinary people accomplishing extraordinary things. We can think about people such as Dr. Martin Luther King Jr. and Mother Teresa, who were ordinary people who did extraordinary things. But let's choose someone a little closer to home. How about Tony Robbins or Jim Rohn?

Tony Robbins is a well-known motivational speaker who is wealthy and has built himself a small empire. But he started out as just an ordinary kid who grew up in a tough situation. His parents divorced when he was seven, and he had to help raise his two siblings. His home life was abusive, and he was banished from the house at knifepoint by his mother when he was just seventeen years old. He worked as a janitor and never went to college. Tony Robbins's life and success are an inspiration.

When you are feeling low, feeling like you can't go on, feeling like quitting, you need to find the stories of other people who have succeeded, and just gobble them up. Read about successful people. Get audio recordings of them speaking. Go and see them live if you can. These don't have to be famous people. You can check out the biographical section at your bookstore and library, or you can just talk to people you meet at social events and ask them about their stories, about how they got to where they are today. Choose people who have achieved what you want to achieve, and let their stories inspire you. If they can achieve their goals, then so can you.

Be of Service to Others

Another way to gain inspiration from others is to be of service to them. Whether you are helping the poor in some way, helping disadvantaged children, volunteering at a hospital to help sick people, or learning about and advocating for the struggles of people in a developing country, these issues can all act as inspiration to us.

We all have something that is important to us, and we all need to give back to our communities. If your child was born with a deformity or illness, it will inspire you to help others who were born with that deformity or illness and perhaps don't have access to the medical care they need. If your family comes from a village in a country that doesn't have clean water, you might be inspired to help that village and other villages like it. If you were injured in a car accident when you were young, you might be inspired to help others who have been through the same type of experience.

The point is that helping and being of service to others is rewarding and will inspire us to continue to grow and develop as people and in attaining our goals so we can give back in ways that are meaningful to us.

Shake Things Up a Little

If you find yourself stuck in a tunnel, then shake things up and run until you see the light at the end of this tunnel. Step out of your comfort zone and try something new. Try a new activity, pick up a new hobby, or go somewhere you have never been. Watch the sunset or the sunrise if you never have before. The idea here is that you may gain a new perspective on life and on your goals and dreams. You may also find some new motivations in the process.

Try to Look at the Familiar in a New Way

Again, this is about perspective. Maybe you just need to look at the same old things in your life in a new way. Take a different route to get to your investment property. Try taking your spouse or friends out to lunch instead of dinner. Watch the sunrise instead of the sunset. Sometimes you can see something you have become accustomed to in a new way.

Take Action

We will talk a lot more about taking action in chapter 8. For now, I will say that taking action inspires more action. Once we gain the momentum of action, it will inspire us to keep moving because it wakes us up from within.

Spend Time in Nature

Believe it or not, even when you are cruising for wealth and riches, stepping back and spending time in nature can help bring perspective, a fresh look at things, and inspiration. Nothing inspires quite like incredible landscapes, vistas, and beauty nature provides for us. We can get so caught up in our pursuit of our goals that we can lose our perspective of what is truly important. We can get so stressed out that we feel overwhelmed. This is when nature is able to soothe and inspires us to keep going.

Meditate

It is important to keep your mind healthy, and meditation will do just that. If you practice mindful meditation, you will find you are better able to stay in the moment. This will make it easier for you to maintain a healthy perspective on life and manage stress better.

Reflection

Take some time to think about what inspires you in life. Write down what comes to mind. Are there any people who have inspired you along your journey? Are there any activities that give you fresh perspective and help you step back and see the world and your place in it differently? Are there any activities you can think of that would help inspire you toward your goal of wealth and success?

Now that you have a solid understanding of motivation and inspiration and how each of these can help you reach the financial success you are striving for, it's time to dig a little deeper. Now it is time to take a look at your thinking. Your frame of mind is critical to your success.

What you do with the circumstances life presents to you will mean the difference between success and failure.

Chapter 6: Think Differently

Very little is needed to make a happy life; it is all within yourself, in your way of thinking.

—Marcus Aurelius

The biggest barrier to achieving financial success or any other kind of success in life is rooted in the way how people think. Surely you have heard all about how you have to think positively. You have heard of the law of attraction. Well, here is the thing. You *do* have to think positively, and the law of attraction does work! "But most people do think about being rich," you say. "Most people decide they want financial freedom and that they want to make changes and make more money. So why aren't more people rich?"

It comes down to *how* you think. There is future thinking, and there is now thinking. Look at it this way. You can sit on your couch and think about being rich. You can desire it and even think of ways you can make it happen. You can come up with a plan and try to follow through with it. You might even set some goals and be positive about reaching them, all the while thinking about how you will be rich one day. This is future thinking—thinking about what you will be and trying to figure out how to make it happen—and it doesn't work.

Huh? This level of positive thinking about what you want to accomplish won't get you what you want? Amazing, isn't it? But really, if just thinking that way was enough to get you what you want, everyone would be a millionaire with a big house overlooking the ocean. There is more to it than just *wanting* something to happen. Let's take a look at now thinking.

Now Thinking

What is *now thinking*? When you think about what you want, decide you want it, and go after it—you have great intentions. But you are thinking like the person you are. You are an average person who has the mind-set of an average person. You will start thinking like a rich person or a successful person when you become a rich and successful person. That just won't cut it.

In order to make your dreams and goals become a reality, you have to think as if you have already accomplished it. You have to have the mind-set that it has already happened. You have to think that way *now*.

In other words, you have to be a success in your mind before you achieve it in reality. How do you do this? By thinking positively. Let's take a look.

Thinking Positively

Back in chapter 4, we discussed visualization. Positive thinking is a good companion to visualization. Theories such as the law of attraction or the power of intention are just ways to explain how positive thinking works and the power it holds. The idea behind positive thinking is really very simple, as these things usually are. Simply put, how you think is how your reality will be. If you think positively, then your reality will be positive, and if you think negatively, then your reality will be negative.

While this concept has been touted for a number of years, it turns out there is scientific evidence to support this theory. First, there are mirror neurons, which are neurons in the brain that cause us to mirror the behavior we see in others. This is why we should surround ourselves with successful people. When we are constantly surrounded by people living as we want to live, we are more likely to mirror their behavior and do what they do to achieve what they achieved.

Another reason to surround ourselves with the people we wish to emulate is that our brains can mirror emotions. There is a part of the brain called the amygdala that taps into the emotional response of other people. That is why we automatically feel fear when someone around us is afraid or feels anxious. We also feel joy when someone around us is happy. Based on the existence of mirror neurons and the amygdala, if we surround ourselves with people who take positive action and exhibit positive emotions, we will also take positive action and feel positive emotions. This will help us make a positive reality. But there's more.

There is a specific region in the brain that is connected to intention. Whenever we have an intention of doing something, this part of the brain becomes active, and it is directly connected to the part of the brain that is responsible for taking action. So if we have an intention, the part of our brain tied to intention will signal the part of the brain that is responsible for taking action so that we take the appropriate action to fulfill that intention.

For this reason, you must have positive intentions. You must decide what you want and focus on that like it has already become a reality. The visualization we talked about in chapter 4 will help, and you will automatically take the action needed to ensure that your intention becomes reality. So how do you set an intention? Here are some steps to follow:

Make a decision. You need to decide on your intention in terms of the person you want to be. In other words, you need to determine *who* you want to be rather than *what* you want to be. You want to create wealth in Dubai. What kind of person is that? *Who* is that? Who will you be if you are wealthy in Dubai? In order to figure this out, you need to take a step back and decide how you can be a different type of person to make your intention become reality. Maybe you need to be a more giving person, rather than looking for ways to take, in order for wealth to come to you. Maybe you need to be content and happy in order to achieve success rather than being anxious and constantly wondering about your future. Decide who you are, and then bring yourself to your intention.

Write it down. Whatever you have decided your intention is, you need to write it down on paper. You can carry it with you or put it on the bathroom mirror so you can see it every day. You also need to repeat that intention to yourself frequently. Say it in the morning when you get up, say it many times throughout the day, and say it before you go to bed. Make your intention a mantra that you repeat to yourself.

Start your day right. Don't just roll out of bed and plug into the world. You need to begin your day mindfully. If you plug into your e-mail, text messages, or social media, you are giving everyone else the power to influence how your day begins. This is not OK. Give the first hour of your day to yourself. Take the time to say your intention to yourself and set your goals for the day based on that intention. Take the time to take care of yourself, whether that means getting in some exercise, meditation, inspirational reading, a healthful breakfast, or sitting with a cup of tea or coffee on the front porch, watching the world wake up. Your day will be better if you start it on the right foot.

Keep track of your thinking. Throughout the day, try to check in with yourself and see what your thoughts are doing. This is particularly important when you start to feel bad, whether it is worry, fear, anxiety, or anger. Whenever you think of it, check in and just become aware of your thoughts. If you wish, you can say a positive affirmation to counter those thoughts.

Pay attention to the words you use. This follows from keeping track of your thoughts. Be mindful of the words you use when talking to yourself and others. Stay away from negative words like should, but, always, never, and hate. Avoid using the word *depressed* to describe yourself or anyone else. And when someone asks you how you are doing, always answer in the positive, even if you don't feel positive. A good, convincing "I'm great" will not only tell someone else you are doing fine; it may just convince you of that too.

Think forward. No matter how much trouble you are having right now, whether that trouble is in your personal life or with your mental health or any other part of your life, you need to move past the idea that you need to fix everything before you can move forward and accomplish your goals. Instead, consider how it would be if you moved ahead with your plans even if everything in your life wasn't pure perfection. What is perfection anyway? Don't know? No one does, because it doesn't exist.

Stop complaining. We talked about this in chapter 2. This is one of the obstacles that get in our way. It is a stinking thinking that needs to go, and it bears repeating here. Complaining is negative, which attracts negativity into your life. Be aware of when you complain. If it is something you can't change, let it go; and if it is something you can change, then do something about it.

Never give up. Never, ever! There will be ups, and there will be downs. There will be times you think your goals are impossible to reach. There will be times when you wonder if you have what it takes or want to make sacrifices to get where you want to be. The answer is yes, you do. You just need to get over this hump, and it will be smooth sailing. Persist, and you will be glad you did.

Reflection

Take the time to consider these steps. Get a piece of paper and a pen and start writing. Sit and think about each of these steps, and write down whatever comes to your mind for the following questions. Just remember that this is a process and you are just beginning it.

- *Who are you, and who do you want to be?*
- *What is your intention? (It's OK to write a few intentions down; you can be more precise as you learn more about yourself.) Write down your intention, and put it somewhere you will see it every day.*
- *How do you start your day? What can you change to have a better start to your day? Can you think of a routine you would prefer? Write it down.*
- *Give some consideration to the thoughts that go through your head. Make a commitment to keeping track of your thoughts.*
- *Take some time to think about your choice of words. Do you frequently use words like never, always, hate, but, or other negative words? Write down words that can replace them, and make a commitment to start using them.*
- *Take some time to think beyond where you are right now in your life. Write down where you are, and then write down where you want to be. Now write down one action you can take today to start moving in the right direction.*
- *Think of something positive you can do when things get tough, a way to help you through it. Write it down, and commit to doing it when necessary.*

Alternative Thinking of Successful People

There is more than thinking positively when it comes to success. That is just one part of the whole. There is also a whole different way of thinking. The expression "out of the box" sounds cliché to say, but it really is just that. Here are the main ways the most successful people think differently from the average person:

They embrace stress. Yes, no matter who you are or what you do, whether you are rich or poor, married or single, a man or a woman, you will experience stress many times in your life. Stress is a fact of life, and the sooner you get with that program, the better. The key that successful people have discovered is that if you see stress as a positive thing, it can help rather than hinder you. In other words, what matters is how we respond to stress. If you see stress as something that is preparing you for what is to come, then there will literally be a shift in your biology, and you will become immune to the effects of stress. This will help you remain calm, be more confident, and have less anxiety, and your cardiovascular health will not suffer the negative consequences normally associated with stress.

They see connections. People very often make decisions based on the moment, without thinking ahead to consider the possible outcomes and consequences or how that decision will affect other aspects of life and future decisions that must be made. The successful person makes decisions in a different way by thinking through the potential connections between that decision and its outcomes and other actions and the consequences of these connections. On the surface, it may not make sense to take out a loan and go into debt, but if that money is invested in real estate and gives you a return that is higher than the initial loan and interest, then it is worth it. That could be the beginning of being able to take the equity from one property and invest in another. And thus you have a chain reaction of good events that began with a decision that, taken on its own, didn't seem practical.

They ask questions. This is so important. Successful people do less talking and more listening. They talk less about themselves and ask questions so they can learn more about others. This takes them out of themselves and allows them to learn more about another person, about a situation, about where they might be mistaken or have gotten something wrong, and about how something works. They value the potential of gaining knowledge over fearing the possibility of looking silly for asking a question. They also get people talking about themselves, which is something people like to do, and this helps them increase their network of friends and contacts, something that is very valuable.

They give without expecting anything in return. Successful people tend to have big hearts. They want to give back to the community in whatever way is most meaningful to them. This helps them to feel fulfilled and helps them develop better relationships with the people around them. Zig Ziglar once said, "You can have everything in life you want, if you will just help other people get what they want." It seems that the key to success is in helping others find theirs. And this giving doesn't have to be on the level of opening an orphanage in India. It can be simple, small acts of kindness that occur throughout the day, such as paying for something for someone at the grocery store when his or her bank card won't work or making fresh coffee for the office before you leave for your morning meeting.

They know curiosity is more important than passion. There is no doubt that passion drives us, but there are a lot of people out there who don't even know what they are passionate about. Curiosity is an innate instinct in human beings. We are curious creatures. If a closed box is left in a room with someone, it may be very difficult for that person not to open the box to find out what is inside it, even if he or she has been told not to open it. The most successful people tend to allow themselves to be curious and to follow that curiosity where it takes them. This is how people find out what is truly important to them— the inspiration that drives them to greatness. It's how they find their passion, and it allows them to run with it.

They schedule downtime. The more you work, the more money you will make, right? Yes, to an extent, but people cannot be on 24-7. The mind needs time to rest, to decompress, to be free of the demands of work. Successful people are well aware of their need for downtime, time when they aren't at the office, time during which they haven't brought the office home with them, and they are turned off in relation to work. It is during these times, when nothing is happening, that creativity begins to surface. In psychological circles, this is known as the incubation period, and it allows our conscious minds to connect with our unconscious minds, which tap into the great flow of information they have at their disposal. Part of success is to schedule time to do nothing to allow the unconscious mind to express itself.

They know experiences are better than material objects. Truly successful people are more concerned with who they are, which they find out through experiences, than what they can acquire. Spending money on experiences rather than things brings people to a deeper level of understanding of themselves and life. Eventually, the material items they surround themselves with are a reflection of who they are rather than the need to have things to show their wealth and status.

Reflection

Consider these different ways of thinking. Do you currently do any of them? If so, it is good for you. Chances are, there are at least a few that you don't do. Choose one of them that you will start working on today. Commit to changing that one aspect of your thinking, and write down how you will make the change, what you will do. Work on it each day until you master it. Then choose another one. Do this until you have worked through all of them.

Remember, this is all about changing how you operate right from the root, from the way you think. As we discussed earlier in this chapter, what you think becomes your reality, so you need to think positively. You need to think in a way that is constructive and spurs you on to achieving great things. Life is determined not by your circumstances but by what you do with them, so make a clear and conscious decision about changing your way of thinking. Everything else will fall into place. Plus, when you change your thinking, you will change your emotions, which is what we discuss in chapter 7.

Chapter 7: Channel Your Emotions

Staying composed, focused, and effective under pressure are all about your mentality. People who successfully manage crises are able to channel their emotions into producing the behavior that they want.

—Travis Bradberry

Up until very recently, the going opinion throughout business circles was that people should keep a cool, calm, and rational head about them. Emotions were something best left outside the boardroom or the office. There was no place for them in the world of business. When investing your money, you needed to think logically rather than letting emotions guide your decisions. But now all this is changing.

More and more, businesspeople and entrepreneurs are realizing the importance of emotions in the workplace. What this means is that it is important to bring emotional awareness into your business dealings because this will help you communicate better, improve your social skills, and promote a positive atmosphere.

But your emotions can also help you in another way. When you are feeling negative emotions, as you are bound to do from time to time when you are working toward your goals of financial success and freedom, you can learn to channel this energy into something good. You can channel that energy into action that will solve your problem or into something that will point you in the direction in which you want to go. We will talk more about channeling your emotions later in this chapter, but first we will begin by talking about attitude.

Attitude for Success

Those who are the most successful in life, regardless of what their achievements are, have a certain attitude that affects everything they do. Yes, their attitudes are positive, but they are also focused on specific ways of thinking that are incredibly constructive. These are as follows:

Gratitude

An attitude of gratitude is important for success, but it has a special significance when it comes to financial success. Gratitude is the act of wanting what you have rather than having what you want. In other words, take stock of what you have, and be grateful for it. And, yes, this means to be grateful for the clichéd things in life such as your health and your family. Be grateful that you have a nice home, that you can afford a car, and that you are well fed. Be grateful for it all.

But gratitude can do more than just make you feel good; it can actually turn into greater financial success. Research has shown that those people who show gratitude for what they have in life have more patience. They have the patience required to say no to the short-term financial gain so they can get more money later on. They have the patience to wait for just the right moment to do something rather than rushing into a decision or an action. In other words, increased patience means better timing, which leads to greater success. And all because they have an attitude of gratitude for what they have in their lives.

Reflection

Many people keep a gratitude list, something they can refer to regularly that will remind them of all the things they are grateful for. This is a fabulous way to recognize what you are grateful for. Create a list of things you are grateful for in your life. Write it on a piece of paper you can carry with you, write it in your journal, or write it somewhere else that works for you. Each day when you get up or when you go to bed or both (preferably), take the time to read over your list. Add to it and adjust it as needed, but review it at least once a day. This will keep your gratitude at the forefront of your mind always.

Empathy

Empathy is the ability to understand what another person is feeling or experiencing from that person's perspective. It's that ability to walk in another person's shoes. Empathy gives you insight and allows you to understand how to best manage and lead people, how to understand what your customers or clients want, and how to negotiate a deal that will be of the greatest benefit to everyone. Empathy is the way you can deeply connect with another person so that you can see things the way he or she does, which will help you develop stronger relationships with the people in your life, even those with whom you do business.

Reflection

Remember in chapter 6 when we discussed the concept of asking questions? Well, this is related to listening to others. From now on, when you have a conversation with someone, do more listening than talking. This means not being just physically present but mentally and emotionally as well. It means not deciding what to have for dinner or whether you should go to a movie. It means not trying to figure out how to respond. Be fully present with the person you are talking to. Commit to listening intently to the next person you speak to and then repeat. In addition to this, always think before you do speak, and consider the impact of what you will say. Choose your words carefully.

Commitment

You must have an attitude of commitment. Commitment can spur you on as much as motivation does, but commitment comes from inside of you rather than from a source outside of you. The best thing about commitment is that it gives you the courage to keep going when you might otherwise give up. This courage will help you take action when you aren't sure you can or should.

Reflection

Take the time to consider what you are on this earth to achieve. Write down your ideas of what your purpose is. If you don't know, then you need to take some time to consider this because it is related to your passion, and this is when your curiosity will hold you in good stead. For each idea that you have written down, write down the things you do each day, and try to connect them to your purpose. If you can't, then perhaps that daily activity should be shed from your schedule. As you home in on your purpose in this life, you will find your level of commitment growing.

Emotional Intelligence

It is extremely important to discuss emotional intelligence here. Again, while there was a time when people thought that emotion was best left outside the workplace, organizations and management all over the world are now realizing that emotional intelligence (EQ) is at least as important as IQ (intelligence quotient). Developing your emotional intelligence is something that will greatly enhance your ability to work with others and develop relationships, which is incredibly important regardless of what type of work you do. It is also important in the world of finance and investment when you are negotiating deals and investing your money.

So what is emotional intelligence? It is a combination of personal and social competence that determines how each of us makes decisions, manages our behavior, and traverses the complexities of our social interactions. In other words, it is a measure of how in touch you are with yourself and with those around you. Below is a breakdown of it.

Personal Competence

Personal competence refers to your ability to be aware of and manage your own emotions and behaviors. It is made up of the following:

- Self-awareness. This is your ability to recognize and identify your emotions and continue to be aware of them as they are happening.
- Self-management. This is your ability to manage your behavior based on your emotions, keep it positive, and adapt it as needed.

Social Competence

Social competence is very similar to personal competence, but your awareness is shifted to the emotions of other people and your relationships with them. The key to social competence is your ability to sense the emotions, behaviors, and moods of the people around you and use that information to inform your relationships with those people. Social competence includes the following:

- Social awareness. This refers to how well you can sense other people's emotions and moods and connect them to what is happening with the person.
- Relationship management. This refers to your ability to take what you know about another person's emotions, your own emotions, and the context in which those emotions exist and use that information to successfully navigate your interactions and relationship with that person.

It is important to understand that no matter how high your IQ is, and no matter how smart or skilled you are, it won't matter at all if you don't have a high emotional intelligence. It has been shown that a high emotional intelligence not only makes a good businessperson but also a good investor. Emotions play a huge role in investment decisions, and research has shown that the investment decisions made by investors don't always make the most sense in terms of their financial success. Instead, they make investment choices based on what makes them feel good.

Having the ability to identify and understand your own emotions and manage those emotions so that you have a clearer picture of how to manage the investment situation is critical to your success as an investor. This also applies to real-estate investing, which is a significant form of wealth generation in Dubai. In fact, when investing in real estate, you have to manage not only your feelings regarding the investment but also your emotions as they relate to the other parties with whom you are negotiating your investment purchase and your relationship with them.

With all of this said, you can develop your emotional intelligence to your benefit. In order to do this, you need to be able to do the following:

Minimize Negative Emotions

This is possibly the most important aspect of a healthy emotional intelligence—the ability to manage negative emotions. If we can't keep these negative emotions in check, we run the risk of their getting out of control and affecting our judgment. When negative emotions are threatening your peace of mind and ability to think rationally, you need to be able to recognize the thoughts that are associated with those emotions and change those thoughts. To do this, try the following:

- Understand and accept that emotions are powerful.
- Understand and accept that because you feel a certain way, that doesn't mean those emotions represent reality.
- To help alter your thoughts, make use of words. Choose words that will negate your emotions, and say them to yourself. For example, if you feel angry about losing an investment opportunity, tell yourself that there are plenty more opportunities waiting for you that are better.
- Make sure your physical needs are met. If you are hungry or tired, you are going to have less control over your emotional state. Make sure you get enough exercise, sleep, and nutrition every day to avoid being moody, irritable, and unhappy. This will help you be more emotionally stable.

Keep Calm and Collected When Stressed

When stressful situations arise, it is important not to cave in to that stress. You cannot avoid stress, so you need to find ways of managing your stress so you can still function and improve your situation. Below are some tips for managing stress:

- Stay away from caffeine because it is a stimulant.
- Avoid smoking and drinking alcohol.
- Learn breathing techniques that will help you stay calm.
- Meditate.
- When feeling stressed, take some time for exercise, even if it's just a walk.
- Splash your face with cold water when feeling stressed. The coolness of the water can reduce anxiety.
- Be social to help you get some perspective.
- Spend time in nature.
- Take time to relax and have fun.

Assert Yourself and Express Negative Emotions When Required

Learn to assert yourself. There are times when you need to set boundaries and times when you need to enforce them. There are times when you need to speak up for yourself and be able to disagree with someone, say no, or otherwise ensure you are being treated fairly. Negative emotions are necessary sometimes, but you need to express yourself in a healthy way. One great approach is to express how you *feel* about a situation because no one can argue with your feelings. You can say, "I feel X when you Y. I need you to Z."

"I feel disrespected when you constantly show up late. I need you to be on time from now on."

"I feel angry when you cut me off when I'm talking. I need you to wait until I'm done speaking before you start."

It takes practice to assert yourself, especially if you have a fear of conflict. But asserting yourself in a respectful manner is important for your emotional intelligence.

Respond to Rather Than React to Difficult People

When a situation occurs that brings about negative emotions, don't react. Reacting is when you let the emotions choose how you deal with the situation. Instead, take a moment to think about the situation rationally before you deal with it. This allows you to respond rather than react. Responding means your rational mind is in control instead of your emotions. In the moment that you take to think, you can do the following:

- Count to ten so that you can calm down.
- Try to empathize with the other person.
- Establish consequences for the person who is being difficult.
- Assess the situation to understand it from all angles.

Express Intimate Emotions with People to Whom You Are Close

If you are going to form connections with people and establish and maintain relationships, then you need to know how to express intimate emotions to those people. This doesn't just mean personal relationships with family, friends, and intimate partners. This also means the kind of relationships you want to build with colleagues, clients and customers, and service providers. You want to establish good relationships with these people, especially if you will be working with them on a regular basis. You can express intimate emotions in the following ways:

- Orally, by saying things like, "How are you feeling?" or "I appreciate what you do for me" or "I'm really glad we work together"
- Through body language, such as patting someone on the shoulder, giving someone a hug, or making positive eye contact
- Through behavior, by picking up coffee and snacks for someone, giving someone a thank-you card, or listening when someone needs an ear

It is very difficult to measure emotional intelligence, or EQ, but there are characteristics and signs that people who are highly emotionally intelligent tend to display. These people tend to be

- curious about other people;
- fluent in a large emotional vocabulary;
- able to embrace change;
- fully aware of their strengths and weaknesses;
- aware of negative self-talk and able to stop it before it gets carried away;
- good judges of character;
- able to say no when necessary;
- difficult to offend;
- able to not hold a grudge;
- able to brush mistakes aside;
- givers, not expecting anything in return;
- buffers around toxic people;
- able to avoid looking for perfection;
- able to appreciate what they have in life and express gratitude;
- able to disconnect from their high-stress lives;
- able to put limits on the amount of caffeine they drink;

- able to get adequate amounts of sleep; and
- able to be joyful despite anyone trying to interfere with that joy.

Reflection

Take some time to consider your level of emotional intelligence. Go through this list of signs of high emotional intelligence, and write down the ones you think you are good at. For each one, write down two examples that show you are good at those things. Next, write down the signs that you don't feel you are good at, and then write down two ways you can improve them so you can increase your level of emotional intelligence. Remember to be completely honest when doing this exercise because if you aren't going to be honest with yourself, you won't get anywhere in life or in your pursuit of financial success and freedom.

Learning to Channel Emotions

Being able to come back after something knocks you down is critical to success because success cannot happen without failure. This is such an important part of establishing a strong emotional intelligence that it is worth talking about in depth.

Let's face it. Nothing in life is ever easy, at least not anything worth having, and sometimes you are in a place in life when you have just been beaten down. Maybe you have made the decision to become rich in Dubai because you are so low in life right now, so broke, that you know you need to make a change and improve your lot. Maybe you thought you had the biggest deal in your life, and something went terribly wrong. Regardless, you need to get out of your slump.

But how can you do that when you feel so bad? After all, we have discussed the importance of being positive, but what happens when you just don't feel positive? Well, all emotions have energy, and while we would prefer the positive emotions, the negative ones are going to show up from time to time. The key here is to take the energy from the negative emotions and channel it into something positive. You can start this process by asking yourself some very important questions:

- Is there a lesson I can learn from this experience?
- Is there a better way I can accomplish this goal?
- What can I do right now to make things better or to change my situation?

This last one is particularly important. If you feel angry at what has happened in life, if you feel envious of what others have, if you feel defeated, or if you feel highly anxious due to your situation, then you need to take control instead of letting the emotion take control. Research has shown that people who start their day feeling negative emotions but who feel positive by the end of the day generally have the highest level of productivity. That negativity, whether it is anger, anxiety, frustration, or envy, kicks people into taking positive action that will result in a change in their life circumstances.

Having said all of this about channeling negative emotions into something positive, this will not happen unless you make a choice to do so. So if you are feeling a negative emotion about something in your life, especially if it is something you feel negatively about on a consistent basis, then you need to make a choice to do something about it. Are you going to wallow in your negativity, or take that energy and do something constructive with it?

Reflection

Get out your journal if you keep one (if you don't, I recommend you do). Look back through it to see if you can identify any negative emotions that tend to occur repeatedly. If you can see this, then try to see if there is a pattern or a common trigger for these instances of negative emotions. If you don't keep a journal, then do the best you can to remember back over the past few weeks or months to find instances of negative emotions.

If you have identified some negative emotions that may be chronic and you know what has triggered them, think about how you can channel the energy of those negative emotions into something positive. Can you take some positive action? Can you stop doing something you have been doing and end a cycle of poor behavior and decision making? If you can't find any instances of negative emotions, then either you are very lucky, or you aren't being honest with yourself.

We have been talking about emotion, how to have a healthy emotional intelligence, how emotion can be good for business and investment, and how to channel the energy of your emotions into something positive. Taking action was touched on, but this is such an incredibly important aspect of success that it is time to discuss how to take action to ensure your success in finding wealth in Dubai.

Chapter 8: Don't Just Sit There—Do Something

Inaction breeds doubt and fear. Action breeds confidence and courage. If you want to conquer fear, do not sit home and think about it. Go out and get busy.

—Dale Carnegie

We have discussed a lot of things in this book, and they have mostly had to do with the mental aspect of success, about how we need to think and feel, about what motivates you, and about how your imagination can help you succeed. But with all of these things, you will achieve nothing without taking action. In fact, all of these mental preparations are intended to help you take action, to get moving, and to make your dreams actually happen—one action at a time.

What it comes down to is that the only way to truly learn and develop and reach your goals is to try. You will learn skills and methods along the journey, but it is only when you try these things that you will know whether or not they will work.

How to Take Action

There are risks and costs to action. But they are far less than the long range risks of comfortable inaction.

—John F. Kennedy

So here is the question: What can you do? If you are sitting there wondering what you can do to move yourself in the right direction, please know there is *always* something that can be done. Even small things can make a big difference. The key here is to just stop thinking and take action. Here is a list of suggestions of actions you can take to move yourself in the direction of financial success.

Set Goals

We discussed setting goals in chapter 5 when talking about motivation. If you haven't already done this, then what are you waiting for? There is no time like the present to set SMART goals for yourself and your business. Decide what you want, set your goal, and then set milestones to make it happen. If you need the capital to get started in investing, then getting a job that will get you started is a great action to take. Or you can see if you would qualify for a loan, provided the loan is a good investment, so that you can buy your first piece of real estate. There are plenty of small actionable steps you can take to reach your goal.

Start Journaling

Chapter 7 suggests keeping a journal. This is a great action to take. You can record the things you are doing in your personal and professional life and the successes and failures you have had. You can also record the feelings and emotions that go along with this. This is a great tool to be able to get everything out and even vent if you need to, but it is also a great way to keep track of your journey. You can always look back to see how far you have come. You can see what worked and what didn't and how you have met your milestones.

Another constructive way to use your journal is as a way to generate ideas. Hedge-fund manager and author James Altucher suggests writing down ten ideas in your journal every day. Some of these ideas might end up being total flops, but others will be successes. Plus, you will be putting out ideas like crazy. You are bound to come up with some real gems that will make you a good chunk of money and help you reach success.

Get Blogging

A companion activity to journaling is to start a blog. Blogging actually shouldn't replace journaling, which is a very personal expression of yourself. Instead, blogging is much more public and is a way to express your ideas, experiences, and opinions to an audience of followers and readers with whom you can create a social relationship via the blog. Blogging is also a super way to establish yourself as a trusted expert in your field.

Participate in Forums

There are plenty of forums out there for people like you, people who want to create wealth and financial freedom. There are even forums that are specifically about creating wealth in Dubai. If you go onto forums and participate openly and honestly, you will meet new, like-minded people. You can ask questions, and you can answer questions. The key is to participate, and you will open doors for yourself. This is also another opportunity to show yourself as an expert in your field or to connect and network with people who are experts and who can act as mentors to you on your journey.

Social Media

You simply cannot do business these days without involving social media in some way. Facebook, Twitter, Instagram, and Snapchat are examples of the most popular platforms. These are fabulous ways for businesspeople to connect with their clients, customers, and colleagues. Through social media, you can really get to know people and establish relationships with them without the involvement of a third party. You can respond to clients and customers directly when they have questions or concerns, and you can directly interact with your followers. This is a great way to market yourself and your business without advertising and without paying a cent. Just remember that you are there to interact with people, not to advertise. Once you have built a relationship with your followers, the rest will fall into place.

Hire a Coach

Depending on your goals, you will choose a coach who is right for you, but hiring a coach can be a life-changing decision. You can hire a business coach or a life coach. Whatever type of coach you choose to hire, you will find that this is not money wasted but an investment in your future. This person can help you get organized, help you get unstuck, and ensure that you are moving in the right direction.

Join a Mastermind Group

A mastermind group is a great way to get the support you need and engage in a community of business peers. These groups are generally invitation only, or you have to apply to join, but it is well worth the effort. The people in your group become collaborators, mentors, and colleagues. You will

- increase your network of business and professional contacts extensively, which will put you in touch with so many people who can have an incredible impact on your business;
- learn new skills and solutions to some of the most challenging aspects of reaching your goals;
- collaborate on new projects together;
- have access to people who can advise you on the best route to take in your business, and you can also help them;
- help one another market and cross promote products and services; and
- see the bigger picture, think out of the box, and stretch yourself beyond the limits of what you knew was possible.

Grow Your List of Contacts

Make it a point to connect with new people or reconnect with old friends and acquaintances every day. Reach out to people you haven't spoken with in months or years. It could be an old high-school chum or a work colleague from five years ago. Try to reconnect with at least one person every day. Whenever you meet someone new, take advantage of it. Ask questions, gather information, and add him or her to your list of contacts. Keep in touch with these people, and establish relationships with them. You will find your network of connections will grow extensively as a result, and you will always have someone to reach out to when you need help or to be there for when they need it.

Hire Help

Hiring an assistant—or, better, a virtual assistant—is a wise move when it comes to maximizing your time. You only have so much time in a day, and no matter what, you can't get more. An assistant can take care of the more tedious and administrative tasks or your business, leaving you to focus on the important things—the money-making things and the things you enjoy doing the most. An assistant is well worth the investment.

Take Care of Your Mind

Your most valuable asset in business is your mind. The sharper and more focused it is, the more you will be able to succeed. Meditating has been scientifically proven to alter the brain so that it is more focused. It also does the following:

- Relieves stress and anxiety
- Improves a number of health conditions such as fibromyalgia and psoriasis
- Helps preserve the brain and keep it from aging as quickly
- Reduces the amount of worry and self-centered thinking
- Is considered by many to be as effective as antidepressant medication
- Improves the attention span and the ability to concentrate
- Helps treat addiction

When it comes to meditation, what is there to lose? There is absolutely nothing that can be lost by doing it and everything to gain. It's that simple.

But Don't Spin Your Wheels

Your life will be no better than the plans you make and the action you take. You are the architect and builder of your own life, fortune, destiny.

—Alfred A. Montapert

People tend to talk a lot about doing something. Have you ever noticed that? They talk a lot about making changes in their lives, in their communities, or in their places of business, but that's all they do: talk. Few people ever actually *do* anything. Why is that? Generally, the timing isn't right for some reason. The circumstances aren't perfect, or they aren't quite ready yet. Sometimes we just like to talk about things we never really want to do that badly simply because it sounds good to talk about them.

You also need to watch out for when you are spinning your wheels. When you are spinning your wheels, you are busy doing things that don't actually produce any sort of measurable outcome. You are spinning your wheels when you do things like make lists, read books, and set up a blog or social-media accounts without actually using them. Understand that these things are important starting points and need to be done, but it's easy to get stuck doing these things because they make you feel busy. But here's the thing: you aren't actually accomplishing anything on your list, doing anything you have read in books, actually writing a blog or posting on social media, or sitting down and starting to write that book until you actually *do* it.

So how do you become a doer rather than a talker? There are a few things you can do to make this happen:

- Set goals (we have already talked about this extensively).
- Actually pick a date on the calendar on which you will stop talking or spinning your wheels and shift into action. Even if you only get a little bit done, it's still action, and you can build on that.
- Set aside time to actually get something done. Make a schedule for taking action, scheduling out the action you want to do and when you are going to do it. If you are going to blog every Wednesday and Sunday, then do it. If you plan to write for an hour every day, then do it. If you plan to purchase your first investment property this month, then do it. It's that simple.
- Tell someone else or do something to make your intentions public. When others know you will be taking action, you are then accountable to someone other than yourself, and it is more difficult to back out.
- Start with one thing you have been talking about doing and take action, but don't try to do too much at once.
- Just stop and actually do something, whether or not you think the timing is right. If you start thinking about why it shouldn't be done right now, stop yourself right away.

- Keep going and try a different approach if you have a setback or a failure.

As with everything else in this book, when it comes down to it, you have choices. You have all this information on taking action, but you ultimately have to choose to do it. No one can choose that for you.

What about Imagination and Positive Thought?

At this point, you may be wondering about what we talked about in earlier chapters. We talked about the importance of imagination and how everything that exists started as a thought in someone's mind. We talked about visualizing ourselves having accomplished our goals. We have talked about thinking positively and thinking as though we are already successful rather than thinking that we are going to be successful. We have talked about having intention. We have talked about how these things will manifest in our lives, but how does this relate to taking action?

These things all trigger in our brains the desire to take action. As we discussed when talking about having intention, the part of the brain associated with intention is connected to the part of the brain associated with taking action. When we think positively, think as though we are already a success, and think with intention, we will automatically take the action we need to take to make it happen.

Just think about it. If you are a successful real-estate investor, how would you act? What things would you be doing each day? How would you dress? With whom would you associate? If you consider yourself a successful real-estate investor, someone who has already achieved your goal of success and wealth, then you will get up every day and dress in a manner that fits that level of success. Why? Because that's just what successful people do. You will make connections with the right people. You will visit potential new properties. You will do the things that a successful real-estate investor would do.

Imagination, thinking, and action are all related. They are interconnected. You can't have one without the other.

Stay Open-Minded

When you are striving to reach your goals and taking the action you need to take, remember not to be so focused on the outcome that you miss the journey. Oftentimes, there will be opportunities that come along that may be of great benefit to you and your overall success, but if you are too focused on reaching the end goal, you may miss these opportunities. Always be mindful of everything going on around you as you journey toward success, and learn to let go of the outcome. This can be difficult to do, but when you can do this, it opens many doors.

Reflection

Take some time to consider the things you have been thinking about doing to become financially successful and acquire wealth in Dubai. Have you been thinking about purchasing investment properties or funding a start-up? Now is the time to take action.

First, choose just one thing you want to focus on. Once you have one thing you are going to do, you will have some time to do the busywork. Plan it out, build a road map, and write down a list of what needs to be done to make it happen. Actually write this all down right now. But don't spin your wheels.

If you have written on your list to get preapproved for a mortgage on a property, then choose a date when you will go into your financial institution or meet with a mortgage broker to get that done. Write down that date right now, and make the appointment. Follow through. If you have written on your list that you will meet with a real-estate agent, then choose a date, and call to set up that meeting. If you have written on your list that you will actually look at properties, then choose a date and set that up.

Whatever you have chosen to do in terms of action, write it down, choose the dates, schedule your time, and make it happen. Do one thing at a time, and when one has been accomplished, act on the next item.

In the end, you do what you can the best that you can, and then you must trust that things will work out. As long as you are taking the appropriate action, even if you start with baby steps, you will find that things will start moving forward, and you will see progress. Once you start taking action, it will result in more action. The ball will be rolling, and you will reach your goals. Success and wealth in Dubai will become a reality.

Chapter 9: Check In

Progress is impossible without change, and those who cannot change their minds cannot change anything.

—George Bernard Shaw

We have covered so much in the pages of this book. It seems like a lot because it *is* a lot. Your effort to be financially successful and gain wealth in Dubai is a journey. Life itself is a journey. The thing about being on a journey is that it is wise to occasionally check in with yourself to make sure that

- you are still going in the right direction;
- you are doing OK and are still healthy, well, and functional; and
- your destination hasn't changed.

If you don't know how you are progressing, how you are doing in relation to the goals you set, then you won't know whether you are on track and doing well. For this reason, you need to check up on your professional progress and your personal well-being.

Checking In with Your Professional Self

The greatest enemy of progress is not stagnation, but false progress.

—Sydney J. Harris

You have a goal. We talked about it in chapter 5, and by now I know you have created one. I hope you have used the SMART technique *and* written it down. Remember the M in SMART? That stands for *measurable*. Part of setting a SMART goal is to make it so that it can be broken down into smaller milestones, each of which has a specific measurable target. This is how you can check in and measure your progress.

The first thing you need to understand is that checking in and measuring your progress is not about beating yourself up if you have gone off track or not reached your targets. It is not about negativity. There is no room for that. Even failure is positive if you choose to see it that way. No, the purpose of checking in and measuring your progress is to adjust your course where necessary so you can keep track of your progress and reach your ultimate goal. With that said, here are some tips to help you check in with your professional progress.

Check In at Regular Intervals

It is wise to check in with your professional progress on a regular basis and at varying frequencies:

- You should do a check-in each day. Checking in at the end of the day is perhaps best, but some people may prefer checking in in the morning. When you do check in, consider the progress you made that (or the previous) day. What went well and what didn't? Did you accomplish everything you wanted both personally and professionally? This is also a time to set your schedule for the coming day. You can set it based on what happened the previous day, allowing you to make small adjustments in your course to help keep you on track to reach your goals.
- Check in at the end of every week. This will give you the opportunity to see each day in relation to the others and determine whether or not you reached your goals for the week. You will also be able to see whether you are on track for reaching the next milestone on your journey and make adjustments if you aren't.
- Check in at the end of every month. This is much like the weekly check-in. You can look back over your month and see how you progressed from week to week. Again, this helps you to see where you might have gone off track, where things worked, and how you might need to adjust your path to stay on task and reach your goal.

Record Your Progress

When you set your goal, you wrote it down in as much detail as you could. However, you should record more than just the initial goal and the milestones. You should be writing down everything you do along the way. The actions you take to reach each of the milestones should be recorded in a journal, notebook, or document on the computer. This way, you will have a record of everything that you did and the outcomes of those actions when available. Remember that this part isn't about analyzing your progress now as much as recording it as you go along so you can analyze it later.

Look to the Past

Even though we are often told not to dwell on the past and that it is important to focus on the future, there is some benefit to looking to the past. When we look back at what has happened, it gives us an opportunity to see what worked and what didn't, where we went wrong, and where we got it right. It is the only true way to measure our progress because progress isn't measured by the relationship of where we are compared to where we want to be; we measure our progress by comparing where we are now to where we were.

Looking back allows us to see the big picture so that we can make adjustments to our course as we keep moving forward. It also allows us to take a moment to see how far we have come and to celebrate our accomplishments. Take the opportunity to celebrate, whether that means taking yourself on a trip or out to dinner (for those bigger accomplishments) or just doing a happy dance. Just be mindful that you don't get stuck looking back. If you continue to look behind you, you can't see where you are going, and you will crash.

Look for Patterns

As you look back over your day, week, and month and see what has worked and what hasn't, look for patterns in your overall activity and conduct. Oftentimes, we can see trends or patterns that made us more productive and others that might have left us less productive. Perhaps when we managed to start our day earlier, we got more accomplished. Maybe starting our day off with exercise gave us more energy to get things started. Maybe we had a habit of procrastinating, which left us accomplishing less. If you can identify these patterns and see when and how you went off track, you can change your behavior to your benefit, making you more productive overall.

Reflection

At the end of each day, week, and month, you should sit down and take the time to look at your progress. Here is an example of what to do each week, but the method is essentially the same for the daily check-in and the monthly check-in. You have written down everything you have done or recorded it in some way so that you have all that information to go through. You will need to read through everything and think about what happened during the week. Take each day at a time and look at the week as a whole. Then you can consider the following:

- *Look at the positives from the week by determining what you accomplished. Did you accomplish everything you had planned to achieve? What made it possible for you to reach these weekly goals?*
- *Look at the negatives from the week. Was there anything that you didn't accomplish that you had wanted to achieve? What stopped you from reaching these weekly goals?*

Once you have worked out the positives and negatives, you can then write out a summary of what happened during the week. This will help you plan for the week to come. It is ideal to create this plan as you are looking back over the week you have just finished. This way, everything is fresh in your mind, and you can plan accordingly.

Checking In with Your Personal Self

Dates that come around every year help us measure progress in our lives. One annual event, New Year's Day, is a time of reflection and resolution.

—Joseph B. Wirthlin

Believe it or not, how you are doing personally has a lot to do with how you will perform professionally. You need to know how you are progressing as a person—how healthy you are on physical, spiritual, and mental levels. You need to know that you are coping well with the potential stress of striving for your financial goals and that you have balance in your life.

Remember Maslow's hierarchy of needs? This is part of why checking in with yourself is necessary. You need to meet those basic needs. Yes, you have your home, and you are well fed and safe, but what about your needs for affection, love, companionship, and belonging? Are you working so hard that you are ignoring these? Are you managing to find time to be of service to others, to contribute to the community, or to pursue a purpose or passion in life?

Life can't all be about work or financial goals, but finding balance isn't always easy. Ideally, you should check in with yourself at the end of each day, at the end of each week, and at the end of each month. Here are a few questions you can ask yourself as part of the check-in process. Answering these will help you know whether or not you are on track on a personal level.

- Are you happy? Well, *are you*? Wealth gives you freedom and the ability to meet your physical needs. Wealth allows you to buy material possessions. But wealth in and of itself cannot make you happy. What you do with your money can help you be happy, particularly if you are spending it on experiences rather than things. The freedom that wealth provides can certainly make it possible for you to pursue the things in life that make you happy. It can help you fulfill your purpose in life. Speaking of purpose…
- Do you have a purpose in life? What *is* your purpose in this life? It isn't to make money and be wealthy. I promise. There is far more to life than making money. As mentioned above, wealth gives you freedom, but freedom to do what? What gets you excited? What gets your motor running? Are you pumped when you get out of bed every day? Of course, we all have our bad days and our down moments, but if you are not energetic and excited about life overall, then you need to give some

serious thought to what all this wealth in Dubai is providing you and what you really want to do in life.

- Are you of service to others? None of us lives in a bubble, and none of us can get by in life without help from others. The ideal is to be interdependent. Plus, being of service to others in some way is very fulfilling in its own right. If you are making progress in reaching your goal of wealth in Dubai, what are you doing with that wealth? Or what are you doing with the time your wealth is freeing up for you? Are you contributing to your community? Are you contributing to the world in some way? How are you helping others? There are so many ways, big and small, in which you can be of service to others. Take the time to consider what is important to you. It can be as simple as volunteering to coach your kid's soccer team or donating money to build schools in developing countries. A feeling of purpose and fulfillment comes from helping others.

- Are you reaching your personal goals? Yes, *personal* goals. You have made professional goals, but what about what you want to accomplish on a personal level? Maybe you want to become a black belt in karate or a skydiver in Dubai. Maybe you want to learn how to play the piano or travel to every country in the world. Whatever your personal goals are, you should treat them the same as your professional goals. Write them down, and make them SMART. See how you are progressing with those goals. These are the ones that will help you feel purposeful. They will help you feel as though you have something to live for.

- How do you feel? This isn't just about happiness. This is about your feeling of calm and peace. How you are feeling includes how you feel physically, mentally, emotionally, and spiritually. Are you tired all the time? Overworked? Stressed? Or do you glow from the inside? Are you thriving in the midst of life? Are you excited about what life has to offer? Take the time to sit quietly and look inside yourself. Feel your body. Check in physically and emotionally. It is easy to ignore it when we don't feel at the top of our game, so this is really important for your overall success in life, even your professional success. It won't matter how much wealth you generate if you have a nervous breakdown in the process. If you find that things are off, do what you need to do to get back on track. Meditate, take yoga or a CrossFit program, eat nutritious meals, and get enough sleep. Make more time for friends and family, to read, or to watch a good movie. In other words, take care of you, not just your business.

Reflection

Take some time to write down what metrics you want to use to measure how you are doing on a personal level. You can use a combination of emotional well-being, physical well-being, and mental well-being. Once you have determined the best ways to measure your overall personal well-being and progress, decide how and when you will check in with yourself each day, each week, and each month. Are you going to do a morning reflection? Or perhaps you will check in at the end of each day. Maybe taking an hour of quiet time every Sunday to reflect on your week and how you have been feeling is a good idea. Whatever you choose to do, write down your plan to check in with yourself, and follow that plan. If you find it doesn't work well, you can change it later, but this way you will have a jumping-off point on your way to total wellness.

Please remember that knowing how you are doing both professionally and personally is very important on your journey to success. Wellness is part of the success mind-set and is a critical piece of the puzzle. Even if you reach your goal of wealth in Dubai, maintaining that success just won't be possible if you are not healthy, whole, and operating at 100 percent.

Chapter 10: It All Comes Down to This

Success is not final; failure is not fatal. It is the courage to continue that counts.

—Winston Churchill

Success is like life; it's a journey. You can achieve whatever you set your mind to if you have the right mind-set. Of course, you have to take appropriate action and see it through, but it's more important to create success in your mind first. With the right philosophy, the use of your imagination, the right motivation, a new way of thinking, and knowledge about how to channel your emotions to produce the results you want, you will have a whole new life.

Throughout this book, I have provided you with reflections. If you have been reading them and doing the work they set out, then you have already taken the first steps to success. I hope you have begun to see the shift in your thinking and the way you see your own journey to success. Here, I offer you one more reflection.

But first, have you ever heard of a mission statement? If so, you have probably heard the term in the context of business. Companies and organizations create mission statements to convey to themselves, their employees, their stakeholders, and the public the reason they exist. The mission statement is what the organization does, for whom it does it, and how it does it. A mission statement should be measurable.

Many companies also create a vision statement that conveys the objectives of the organization—the type of future the organization desires. These objectives will help to guide the decisions made by the organization and the actions it takes.

The wonderful thing about mission statements and vision statements is that they can be personal. A personal mission statement and a personal vision statement will guide you through your journey to success and wealth, keeping you focused on your values and objectives along the way. When creating a personal mission statement and a personal vision statement, you need to do the following:

- Identify and list successes you have had in the past.
- Determine your core values.
- List the various ways you can contribute to the business community, your local community, your friends and family, and the world.
- Determine your goals in life.

This information will give you what you need to write your mission and vision statements and make them strong. An example of a personal mission statement might be, "To invest in properties that can be used to provide affordable housing for everyone who needs it."

When it comes to writing a personal vision statement, you need to consider what you want to achieve and what your objectives are. For instance, if you consider the mission statement given above, then perhaps a suitable vision statement would be, "A world in which everyone has roofs over their heads and beds to sleep in."

Now it's your turn.

Reflection

Take some quiet time to reflect and consider your personal mission statement and personal vision statement. If you have already done the reflection exercises in this book, they have set you up for this, and if you haven't yet done them, then you will find this is a great starting point from which to dive into the rest of the reflections.

Mission statement: Determine why you exist as a person and as a professional. Create one sentence that combines these personal and professional reasons for your existence into a mission statement you can use daily.

Vision statement: Decide on your objectives, what you want to achieve in your personal and professional lives, and how this relates to your values. Come up with one sentence that combines these into a vision statement that will guide you.

You can adjust these personal mission and vision statements if they change over time. Just create them, and whenever you feel like you are losing your way, please take the time to read them. In fact, you should read them every day and post them in your office where you can always see them.

Like the journey of life, writing this book has been a journey—a great one. I hope you have enjoyed taking this journey with me, and I wish you all the luck in the world as you journey toward wealth and success in Dubai. You can do it. Just remember: in your mind, you already have!

www.ingramcontent.com/pod-product-compliance
Lightning Source LLC
LaVergne TN
LVHW011411080426
835511LV00005B/474